A Tropical Odyssey

A Tropical Odyssey

To Harriet
with my best wishes
Robin Bryant

Robin Bryant

Memory Lane

First published in Great Britain by Memory Lane
ISBN 978-0-9566518-8-4

Printed and bound by Good News, Ongar, England.

Contents

Preface	 1
The Tropics	 3
The Russells	 11
Levers Plantations	 15
The Bank Line	 21
A Five Minute Strike	 25
Washing By The River	 35
Flying In The Solomon Islands	 39
Rebecca	 43
Yachts and Visitors	 47
The Hybrid Coconut Palm	 49
Independence 1978	 53
We Leave The Solomons	 57
A Muddle In Samar 1980	 59
Manila and Music	 67
A Year of Nil Achievement and Hope	 71
A New Beginning	 75
Under Surveillance	 81
The Greeks of Kunduchi	 85
A Huge Success - First Stage	 93
Diversions	 97
Mixed Fortunes	 103
Schooling Becomes a Priority	 107
Back to the East	 111
To Jacobobad	 117
Transmigration	 123

Muara Wahau and Sangkurilang 127

The Schemes 131

Christmas 1990 139

How Not to Renew a Contract 147

Sarawak 151

Union with Malaya 155

SADP 1992 161

The Interior 163

The Mountains 169

The Plan 177

Music and the Hash House Harriers (HHH) 179

PNG and the Rascals 183

Collingwood Bay and Kokoda 187

A Detour 193

Kwamtili Estate 201

The Last of the Veterans 209

Subsistence Farming in Indonesia 215

Pollution Over Ambon 221

Evacuation by Mission Air 223

Presidential Elections 229

A World Bank Mission 235

Back to Africa 239

Bottoms Up 243

Preface

After seventeen years working for Harrisons and Crosfield in Malaysia as a plantations manager, described in Fading Pictures, I was recruited by Unilever in 1978, to manage their Solomon Island properties.

Julia, my wife, and I left Malaysia with mixed feelings. Was it a sensible move to change companies, countries, lifestyles and friends? Anyway, the die was cast and the contract signed and sealed. The umbilical cord which joined us to Malaysia was now irrevocably broken.

I stayed three years with Unilever and then embarked on a career as a consultant on tropical tree crop agronomy.

During this period, the 1980s and 1990s, agricultural development in the tropics attracted considerable interest and support, particularly from the World Bank.

Thus for many of us with a plantation background, numerous career opportunities arose and for the next twenty years I travelled the world, accompanied by Julia, when working on the longer duration projects, and our children, should school holidays permit.

Consultants during those days were generally hands-on operators; individuals used to working on their own, providing advice, recommendations and management skills to government extension services, to farmers and estate managers. Smelling the soil, assessing the land's economic viability, drawing up plans and budgets and planning for the future.

During the tropical evenings, computers being a rarity, everything was handwritten or typed. Sweaty brows and fingers, late evenings,

1

buzzing mosquitoes. Reports, programmes compiled, planning for the next day, farmers eager to gain a new insight into a crop or a cow. Meetings and seminars, full of farmers listening, seeking a niche market which would make them rich.

A few of the projects were a waste of time and effort. Some were just not successful due to natural causes. The hybrid coconut programme in Tanzania an unfortunate example, when unproven progeny, drought and pestilence played havoc.

However thousands of smallholders and peasant farmers to whom the funds and assistance were designated did benefit considerably.

Once, when attached to a cashew nut project in the Philippines on the island of Palawan, I promoted the crop through a film show and then a series of descriptive slides to eager farmers. After the seminar one old man came over and congratulated me on my presentation.

'You spoke just like President Marcos used to,' he exalted, 'like you, he spoke without notes.'

Mr. Marcos had fled the country accused of corruption and misgovernment.

I did not have to flee a country. Almost, but not quite. I felt privileged to participate in a way of life I loved, unique in its exclusiveness, with no petty rules or bureaucratic constraints to question my involvement in the tasks I was assigned to undertake.

It was indeed a tropical odyssey and for the current crop of tropical agriculturists, if there are such beasts around, such opportunities no longer exist, for the job has changed.

Economists and computers have taken over. No consultant is suntanned; all are spoilt with plush living. Institutional building is the subject, just look at the logos on their smart 4 x 4 vehicles.

The kid in the office block has taken over.

1

The Tropics

To find the real world of the tropics, look south of Timbuktu a degree or two, and draw a line encircling the globe east to west and equidistant from the equator. Then get into your boat or your flying machine and journey south until you reach the more temperate regions of the globe where glaciers sparkle and noisy colonies of penguins strut their stuff upon snow and ice. Then you know you are no longer in the tropics and anyway you will have passed through the warmth barrier and should be feeling fairly chilly.

That is it, a vast area of desert, rainforest and savannah; of magnificent flora, entwining vines and flowering orchids, inhabited by wild beasts, fierce and passive, encompassing three vast continents, South America, Sub-Saharan Africa and the Far East.

*****

Should you be fortunate to have experienced life in the tropics for any length of time, then it is probable you will want to go again or, if you happen to live there, it is unlikely that you will ever want to leave.

It is so easy to become assimilated to the warmth, the soft ambience of life and the delicious awakening scents of the tropics which quickly enter your blood, course your veins, an addiction to embrace and be embraced. Eventually the tropical experience complements both sides of your being, making obsolete the suffocating conformity of the West with its million petulant rules, while at the same time acknowledging the bequeathed ancient values of justice and fair play, respected by all except, sadly, less frequently in the Tropics, much to the anguish and grief of the native people.

When I was a boy in the 1950s much was already known of those far off regions, as information became more accessible through wireless broadcasts and newspaper reports. Perhaps, also, encounters with persons who lived and worked in the tropics. At school, recruiters extolled the virtues of serving overseas as police officers or as colonial administrators; Glubb Pasha promoted his Bedouin Arab forces in Jordan as a career opportunity.

From second hand bookshops in English towns turgid tales of competing tough, resolute explorers could be purchased for a shilling, a few pence extra if there were graphic pictures to complement the stories told within. And maps, colour coded to show which country had been colonised and by whom, priding ourselves on those coloured a pinky red; our collection of countries over the centuries.

At the cinema newsreels showed fighting in Malaya between the British and Malayan troops on one side, against the Chinese communist terrorists, the baddies backed by Mr. Mao Tse Tung, on the other. Probably on the same newsreel the French were shown being pushed out of Vietnam, as were the Dutch from Indonesia. Crying families distraught at airports, hating to leave but no longer welcome, presented a woeful picture.

However happier scenes of vast awesome lands inhabited by jolly people, often cavorting before a plume-hatted visiting dignitary, sparked in me a lively interest. The tropics must also be fun I thought.

*****

In actual fact it was my father who, becoming exasperated at my dithering when searching for a life after agricultural college, pushed me into the clutches of a plantation company, Harrisons and Crosfield Ltd, located in the City of London. They agreed I possibly could fit the bill as a rubber planter. What they were looking for in their selection process I knew not, but I was accepted.

I looked up rubber in an encyclopaedia and then trees, and then an author who might know about both and the life of a rubber planter in Malaya. That was not difficult to find as Somerset Maugham had written many poignant tales of dissolute planters living in splendid, exotic, steamy isolation on estates, lounging about on rattan furniture served by honey-coloured maidens with flowing black hair.

This all sounded splendid and, after signing an agreement which stated that I was not allowed to return nor marry until my first tour of duty, four years, had been completed, I departed for Liverpool and there caught a boat to Singapore, arriving one month later, in September 1961.

*****

I spent 17 exceedingly happy years in Malaya, later to be called Malaysia. However there comes a stage in one's life when you search around and feel that it is time for a change of some sort or other. Marriage, for example, just done, for Julia née Favell from Penberth, Cornwall and I were married in 1976 after a five week courtship; divorce therefore unlikely, a new career or a different venue, possibly. At the same time leaving the tropics was also not an option for us; it would be sufficiently heart-wrenching to leave Malaysia should the time ever come.

Well the time had come as I was approached by Unilever, a food and soap manufacturer, to manage their coconut estates in the Solomon Islands, a few minute specs in the Pacific an inch or so north east of Brisbane (Australia), on the map.

Julia and I discussed what to do next.

'Accept,' she said, 'or we will be on this estate forever.'

'There will be no music in the Solomon Islands for you,' (she was a professional musician) 'and the people will definitely not be like the Malays, Chinese or Tamils of Malaysia.'

With considerable misgivings we departed Malaysia in 1977 and returned to the U.K. to find out more about the offer.

*****

I was lucky to be offered another job, for many friends and acquaintances who had either retired or been retrenched after decades of honest endeavour soon realized that the hostile environment of snarling traffic, endless shopping excursions, cold, damp skies and that singly unpleasant duty of entertaining smelly, snuffling adenoidal infants, or, worse, grandchildren, thrust upon them by grateful parents so that they could enjoy an evening out, alone, without their offspring bawling, strapped into the rear seats of their Fiestas, was not a particularly appealing way of spending one's retirement, whether it be semi or permanent.

Thus a few months of homeland servitude was enough for many. C.V.s were dusted down, companies phoned, enquiries made. 'Yes, I am very adaptable. Borneo, up a river, fine. Sounds like paradise,' they think.

'What are you doing?' I phone an ex-planter friend, recently retrenched.

'I'm in bed,' he replies. 'It is too cold outside.'

'I know it is,' I say soothingly, 'but you can't stay in bed forever.'

A short sharp bark of laughter follows, 'Only another two weeks and I am then off to Pekanbaru' (Sumatra, Indonesia), 'thank God,' he enthuses. 'I am rejoicing,' he continues, 'I have had enough! Enough!' he shouts down the telephone. 'And you?' he asks, 'and what are you doing?'

'I am off to the Solomons,' I reply.

'What luck to go there,' he compliments me.

Before Julia and I leave for the Solomons I phone his house and speak to his wife. She confirms he has vanished to the tropics.

'Pekanbaru?' I query.

'Oh no he is in Papua, New Guinea, I think,' she answers.

*****

Indeed I felt very fortunate. The agricultural world of the tropics was changing. Western governments and aid agencies were becoming increasingly involved in aiding the undeveloped and poor countries of the third world. The rich nations were being persuaded to invest money in agriculture, through the World Bank and others, to provide an agrarian base, a launching pad to prosperity.

They need assistance, pleaded the United Nations. A better lifestyle and improved incomes breed stability. The West holds the pot of gold, while the undeveloped world owns the land. 'We must help', became a familiar cry.

Far the next 25 years governments and aid agencies ploughed considerable resources into agriculture projects. At the same time plantation companies continued to develop and expand but were now recruiting local planters rather than expatriates. Those days were going, almost gone.

*****

My interview with Unilever was a much more pleasant affair than eighteen years previously when I first entered the archaic domain of Harrisons and Crosfield. The Executives of Unilever's plantation group appeared kind and considerate and I was even wined and dined upstairs in the executive suite. It all appeared to be a step up the career ladder.

After learning a little of plantations group activities worldwide I signed a contract and after four days of travel from London via Brisbane Julia and I arrived in the Solomon Islands tired and grubby.

Honiara, the capital, is sited on Guadalcanal Island, renowned for the very vicious battle which occurred when the Japanese invaded the island and were repulsed by the American Marines at the battle of Bloody Ridge.

7

Strewn about the seabed surrounding the islands is a plethora of Japanese and American warships and planes. Here naval engagements decided the fate of the Pacific islands as both the American and the Japanese armies tried to wrest control of the thousands of islands which dot this vast ocean, the Pacific

A large fenced off portion of this famous ridge and the extensive undulating plains beyond, up to the jagged hills in the distance where gold had been found, was now being ranched by Lever's. However the company's interest in developing the land intensively was inhibited by the many unexploded shells which littered the landscape.

The Australian manager of the property, Lunga Estate, John Huysee, met us and, rather than suggesting we stayed longer on Guadalcanal, put Julia and me on the inter-islands airline which would drop us off at Lever's HQ, at the Yandina settlement on the Russell Islands, a forty minute flight away.

*****

Air turbulence by mid afternoon in the Pacific is more than just robust and, although we climbed in the small eight-seater to 7,000 feet, the flight was exceedingly bumpy. Likewise our landing at Yandina airstrip would have been considered unacceptable anywhere else, for we hit the runway with force and then bumped up into the air again. The Australian pilot, usually all were inexperienced or failed Quantas or Ansett aircrew, gathered control and we touched down more sedately.

The pilot apologized for the bumpy landing, must have been the crosswinds, he excused himself. Which was not strictly accurate as the Americans had laid the Yandina runaway during World War II for their bombers and therefore ensured it was aligned in the direction of the prevailing winds. And the runway was very long indeed. In fact our little airplane could have bumped up and down at least six times, and even then there would have been runway to spare.

Anyway, we were now safely down on Lever's property and taxied up to a neat wooden terminal hut with a thatched roof of palm fronds, set amongst the coconuts which fringed the runway.

'Welcome to Yandina,' called the pilot from the front, 'I am sure we will meet again soon as you fly the Islands', he chuckled.

'Yes indeed,' I replied, and then under my breath to Julia I vowed never to fly Solomon Island Airlines unless I was sitting alongside the pilot. As I had in 1967 passed my flying exams in Malaysia and while in U.K. obtained my British pilots licence, the next step was to acquire a Solomon Islands licence post haste, which I duly managed. I wanted my finger hovering over the joystick when I was visiting Lever's properties by plane.

We were met by the senior staff, all Australians, the Financial and Company Director Jim Broom, a Canadian, was on leave, and a variety of Solomon Islanders, amongst them two staff members, Kerosene Jim and Davidson Fekau who were valuable members of the community and also excellent rugby players, a game much enjoyed by the Islanders.

We had arrived and were driven through groves of swaying coconut palms to our bungalow sited close by a coral beach. A most exquisite setting.

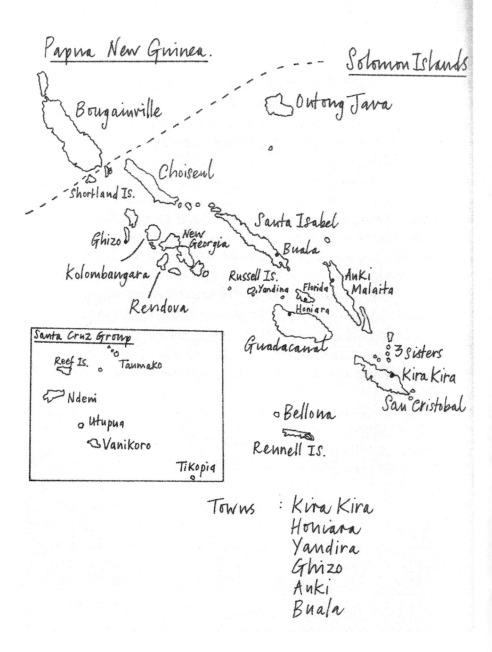

Papua New Guinea.
Solomon Islands

Bougainville
Outong Java

Choiseul
Shortland Is.

Santa Isabel

Ghizo
New Georgia
Buala

Kolombangara
Russell Is.
Auki
Malaita

Rendova
Yandina
Florida

Honiara

Santa Cruz Group

Reef Is.
Taumako

Guadacanal
3 sisters

Kira Kira

Ndeni
San Cristobal

Utupua

Vanikoro
Bellona

Rennell Is.
Tikopia

Towns : Kira Kira
Honiara
Yandira
Ghizo
Auki
Buala

2

The Russells

Mr. Lever, of soap fame, while journeying around the world looking for possible sources of vegetable oil, swam ashore when visiting the Russell Islands, a small group of coral islands northwest of Guadalcanal. Having avoided the sharks and the ferocious Islanders he decided that this was the place to develop his oceanic empire and grow coconuts to supply the Lever soap factories in Liverpool, in which the oil was so necessary for its manufacture.

As this all took place 100 years ago, bureaucratic protocol was limited to persuading the locals to hand over the land on payment of a few axes, nails, hammers and machetes, in additon to a variety of glittery baubles purchased from cut price stalls close to Liverpool docks. These were sufficient enticement for the natives of the Islands to release their most fertile portions of land, and a deep water lagoon which would provide safe harbour for ships to enter and go about their business.

The process of procurement was simple and, once the island's leaders had scratched their names upon the contract of sale, which in most probability none could decipher, Mr. Lever departed the islands leaving his planters to set about creating a coconut empire, firstly on the Russells, then later on other coral bumps within the Solomon's archipelago.

*****

My arrival in late 1977 was just another episode, minor indeed, in

Outside our bungalo at Yandina

the company's commercial advancement.

At the time a large-scale replanting programme of the plantation's 100 year old senile palms was just beginning and hybrid coconuts were now being used for the first time as commercial planting material. It was estimated that production would double by planting these wonder palms.

The company had also been busy establishing cocoa as an intercrop of the coconuts. World Bank calculations predicted that, owing to the current favourable price, cocoa could be considered a commodity crop of considerable potential for the estates to grow. And, because there still remained large tracts of unused land beneath the coconut palms, cattle were introduced to roam freely and graze without interruption, thereby providing a lucrative source of beef.

*****

Indeed the Russells were a paradise, Mr. Lever had chosen wisely. Many visitors considered the island group to be the most beautiful in the Solomons. Extensive reefs harbouring exotic coral life surrounded the islands and the seas teemed with fish. Sharks and barracuda glided past our doorstep, fifty metres away, making swimming hazardous. Turtles periodically trundled on shore and were hungrily sought after by the workers who lived in camps close by.

No flotsam or jetsam littered the shores; no plastic bottles or bags, nor jettisoned rubbish from passing vessels. Not a single tin can was visible. Effluent and soiled garbage were unknown. The sea was pure and clear, completely unspoilt.

Everybody dreams of living on a Pacific island, the great escape, so eagerly sought after but seldom realised. How lucky we were, unimaginable to most, and I was being paid to live and work there amongst the palms, within the boundaries of the coral and shaded by the casuarinas trees and hibiscus which thrived on the coral sands.

So different to Malaysia, but only to be expected. Malaysia was also very beautiful, with its central spine of jungle-clad mountainous terrain, idyllic villages, velvet green rice fields and sandy gentle sea shores.

Beautiful people, calm and assured, clever and industrious, ambitious. Such descriptions, in all honesty, eluded the pleasant mix of Melanesians, Polynesians and Micronesians who inhabited the Solomons. For although they had many qualities, charm and beauty did not come quickly to mind. Nor did they compare favourably in their ability to pick up the latest technology which was now increasingly becoming available.

But then one cannot expect a people living in such an isolated but fruitful environment to be interested in other concepts of life when everything for daily use was so easily gathered from around them.

The pace of life on the Islands was exceedingly slow. Colonized by the British in 1893, the day to day running of the islands was left to a consortium of elderly leftover colonials and ex-council workers from Brisbane, a concoction that hardly could be described as either inspiring or progressive.

A futuristic vision of the Solomon Islands never entered the equation. Independence was to be granted next year, how were the islands going to survive? Planning nil, muddle-headed ideas thought up by ill-educated grey public servants, many with moderate socialist leanings gleaned from left wing suburban town halls whose notion of development centred around a policy of nationalisation and which therefore included all the major sources of wealth creation, namely Unilever Timber, Lever's plantations and the Commonwealth Development Corporation's properties (CDC). A fish canning factory was being operated by the Japanese and gold had been recently discovered in the mountainous region of Guadacanal: Solomon Islands Airlines was the fourth largest company. 'Who else?' they asked themselves.

Fortunately any debate on the country's future, however vague, was confined to the Yacht Club or the comfortable veranda of the Mendana Hotel in Honiara and solemnised over long, delicious draughts of Castlemaine beer, sliding down eager throats.

The islands had drifted too long, 'What next?' 'What to do?', 'Oh, thank you, I don't mind if I do,' as another beer is slid along the bar to be grasped by an eager hand, blotched and freckled through drink and sun.

3

Levers Plantations

Mr. Lever, after acquiring the Russells, left later discoveries and acquisitions to the company's administration, which was put into place as the islands became a collection of disciplined estates. New properties were sought. In the north the Unilever logging company had taken over the island of Kolombangara and denuded it of all its hardwood.

In Honiara the colonial officers were appalled and critical, but could do little about it because the company's taxes were essential for the progress of the country. In their embarrassment, Unilever 'logging' facilitated the introduction of agricultural projects and a coconut plantation was established.

On Guadalcanal, the main island of the Solomons, cattle ranching on the plains and around Bloody Ridge provided a ready source of meat for the capital, Honiara. Further north at Rua Vatu, past the prison camp, the Commonwealth Development Corporation's oil palm estates and the Government's Agricultural Research Station, a small coconut plantation had been established on grey sandy soils, abundant harvests of high-grade copra processed.

And then, to the far south, past San Cristobal, to the last outpost of Unilever's empire, the Three Sisters Islands Estate. Deep vast seas bludgeoned the coastline and access was only by seaplane or by boat, should the seas be calm.

It was a tale of distances and access. For the government, Lever's was a major source of tax revenue, it provided employment to the

Islanders and, even in the remotest areas, ensured a flow of cash into the local economy. However it became increasingly obvious that although the price of copra was at an all time high and cocoa prices were nearing £3,000 ton, productivity would have to be increased for the company to survive. The company's overheads were enormous and the actual manday output low compared to other countries growing tropical crops on an industrial scale.

*****

Effective management of the company's workers was essential but often lacking; all estate managers, except on Guadalcanal, were Solomon Islanders. Some were local, others came from the outer islands, who at some stage had been to school and were considered to have man management potential. Most were uneducated, although big men amongst their tribal group.

The most senior manager was Davidson Fekau from Tikopaia. Well educated and a bull of a man who on one special occasion was invited to attend a garden party at Buckingham Palace. As there was no suitable clothing for sale in Honaria his measurements were sent to a tailor in Hong Kong, who on receipt of the telegram detailing his size, replied by return requesting confirmation that the sizes written down were indeed correct, for no Chinese tailor could comprehend that the neck size, chest, waist and hips could be exactly the same. He cut a splendid figure when the suit eventually arrived, and off he trotted to meet the Queen. He was suitably impressed with Buckingham Palace but was quite surprised that the lawns appeared not to be grazed.

David F. was manager of Pepasala island's estate, an hour away by canoe and most of the workers were Tikopaian, recruited from their homelands on the outer islands. They worked in family groups to extract the copra, the white albumen of the coconut, and would deliver daily over a ton per family during the peak cropping season. The Tikopaian male and female would smoke their pipes contentedly while

16

Cutting copra

working, the females mostly topless.

The most aggressive and certainly the best copra cutters came from Malaita, an island people known for cannibalism in the past and who were responsible, not so long ago, for repeatedly eating out the Isabel Islanders, who were much gentler and whose features were considered more attractive due to their intermingling with visiting Spanish sailors in centuries past.

We recruited Malaitans whenever possible to fill our labour requirements. They were generally more hardworking than other Islanders, and were particularly powerful around the shoulders and arms. Kerosene Jim was a good example. Born and cradled in a sliced

17

down 200 litre oil drum he was strong and bright and after serving as an apprentice book-keeper became elevated to headman. He was one of my favourites and eventually was made manager of a small estate.

Their physical strength on occasions could be prodigious, as I observed when Bert the Australian bulldozer driver got the road grader stuck in a roadside drain after heavy rain. Arriving at the scene I suggested to the foreman that he send one of the Fijian drivers to go and fetch a bulldozer to pull out the grader. The nearest bulldozer, he replied, was at the far end of the island, it would take too long. Then mustering every man, woman and child in the vicinity, they pushed pulled and dragged; the mud slurping around the grader, sucking it down while logs of wood were stuck beneath as they moved it inch by inch upward. Some of the crowd, in their efforts, disappeared underneath the grader, the mud swallowing them up; thankfully, then surfacing slimily, laughing and enjoying the whole episode. How the Islanders loved the physical side of their lives. An epic feat of strength the like of which I have never seen since.

*****

The only problem with the Islanders from Malaita was that after earning very good salaries for a few months work they would then suddenly depart and return to Malaita.

I was at the wharf one evening when the island hopping steamer arrived to unload passengers and cargo before returning to Honiara or wherever was the next port of call.

'Why are so many leaving?' I asked the harbour master, Andifekau.

'They are returning to their island where they belong,' I was told. 'Work too hard here,' he continued.

'But they earn very good money,' I replied.

'Oh yes and now then go back along one talk' (relatives, friends) 'and build house and findem woman. No worry they will come back.'

Indeed they did return a few months later, but it was difficult to manage a plantation when periodically a quarter of the work force would suddenly, without warning, catch the next boat out.

Jim Broom, the Finance Director, who was married to a Fijian called Peggy, being master of the plantation's finances, would spend many hours trying to hatch up schemes on how to keep the labour on site.

We built more houses, very nice ones too, and a social centre, which eventually become a popular beer hall. We increased cutters' wages, but that caused problems with the government whose own wages for unskilled or semiskilled work would no longer be competitive. A hospital assistant grade I was recruited as many outer Islanders brought malaria to the Russells. We even employed prisoners from the local police jail, and there were many, which was a popular move, as the police then had no need to be responsible for their welfare. And, provided no other restrictions on their movements were deemed necessary, all that was required was that they should appear in front of a magistrate or his designate occasionally to confirm their good behaviour. As this was either Jim or me, the scheme worked exceedingly well, and the prisoners, usually held over for drunk and disorderly offences, preferred the freedom of the estates than the cell, for they hated being incarcerated behind bars.

On one occasion a group of workers became drunk and riotous in the copra factory; the main offence, dancing on the rows of diesel powered copra dryers to the beat of a drum. When I arrived the police were trying to round them up, but being only two in number they were outflanked and the drunks continued their ¬leaping and dancing. Eventually, after one had been knocked down and the exercise had sobered the rest, they were taken off to the police station and locked up in the three vacant cells, later to be released to cut copra.

Violence was certainly not a common feature of an Islanders' character, but drinking beer was very much enjoyed and, once imbibed in excess, tempers could quickly fray. Drink however could not be banned, it was a pleasure which everybody enjoyed and Castlemaine beer on payday was drunk in large quantities. Most employees were sensible and drank with their friends in the evenings, in their homes or outside under the shade of the flame trees. In order to try to encourage the workers to spend their money on more worthwhile objects, Jim persuaded the local shops to bring in bicycles for sale, pots and pans, different styles of clothes. Needless to say this exercise in upmarket commercialism received little support. Tatty shorts, Australian Rugby League emblazoned singlets, tobacco and beer continued to be most in demand. Little else grabbed their attention.

4

The Bank Line

The big day of Levers calendar was the visit of a Bank Line cargo vessel to Yandina to take off the copra and cocoa. Islanders paddled their canoes from afar to watch and enjoy the visit of the ship, hoping to buy the odd luxury that a crew member might sell, or, explore in and around should they be recruited to assist in its loading. Never to filch a keepsake, that was taboo, but just to experience another floating world. The event had a carnival atmosphere.

Just as the skies were filled with turbulence, so the seas surrounding these coral islands were fraught with obstacles. Jagged reefs and angry currents sweeping over narrow shoals necessitated captains to be skilled in their navigation.

Accidents happen, they are inevitable, one just has to limit their frequency. However when accidents do occur in isolated locations such as on a Pacific island, the repercussions are much more severe. For the logistics of overcoming a major or minor disaster is magnified by the complication of huge distances between minute specs of land in an immense sea.

My first experience of a Bank ship visit was hardly auspicious. From far off the gathered workers and villagers watched the cargo ship emerge above the horizon before passing close by the outer islands. Kerosene Jim remarked on its speed, for the ship seemed careless in its approach by not observing either the buoys or the pilot markers strategically placed to ensure safe passage. Around the protruding headland of the lagoon the vessel charged; massive, dwarfing the coastal fringes. Closer and closer she surged and then suddenly there she was, this towering metal beast bearing down on Lever's godowns and harbour complex. The wharf buckled on impact, the heavy steel girders screeched and gnashed as if in pain.

Elevators, cranes, and tractors were tossed aside and the watching throngs fled to a safer distance. Amongst them was Ron Hutt, the engineer, whose fleet nimbleness, unnoticed for fifty years, excited much comment when later draughts of beer were being downed in pubs and clubs and endless stories of how the Bank Line destroyed Lever's wharves flowed to and fro.

Engines clanged into reverse, the Captain peered over the ship's bridge wiping sleep from his eyes and took control. The ship backed away from the folded wharf and edged out into the centre of the lagoon and dropped anchor.

A red-faced Captain and First Mate bustled ashore cursing. Jim and I arrived. Bystanders returning to the scene were now thoroughly enjoying the spectacle, gleefully chuckling and pointing at the damage, spitting betel nut juice and tobacco wad onto the ground and uttering facetious comments about, big man (Captain) along ship now in plenty trouble, and gurgling with delight as the Captain stepped ashore, trying to appear unconcerned and in control. 'Oh dear, apologies, who was in charge on the bridge?' embarrassed glances, 'First time it has ever happened,' 'Bloody stupid midshipman.' Compensation claims, sackings and mental breakdowns in the offing.

Jim and I tut-tutted sympathetically, Ron Hutt frowned, long nights ahead, and muttered that he had never seen the like before. Not helpful, but true. As we possessed a landing craft, plus tugs and cargo lighters, we put these immediately into service, and as night fell and the lights from the ship and the wharf played upon our Dunkirk Armada of landing craft and lighters, the sacks of dried copra and cocoa were slowly barged out and loaded into the ship's hold.

This was going to take time but the drama meant that there was no lack of recruits to supplement the wharfees as the double-handling of the cargo and the baking hot conditions in the hold took their toll upon the fitness of the slaving labour.

Of course the Bank Shipping Line paid for the construction of a new wharf and was also obliged to pay the difference for normal loading and the extra labour required to manhandle the cargo post wharf destruction. In the end Lever's got a brand new pier and elevators and, as Jim succinctly drawled six months later, 'Well Robin would you believe it? We made a profit!'

It was always of considerable interest to me that whenever Levers Solomons suffered a calamity of some sort or other that once Jim had been let loose on it the company would eventually benefit, although incidences were fortunately infrequent. When they did occur, Jim would come bounding along to my office and say, for example, 'You know that cyclone off San Christobel that hit Three Sisters estate? Well would you believe it, insurance have paid up for the three lighters plus cargo which were wrecked.'

'Wrecked?' I shrieked, 'Nobody mentioned that our lighters got wrecked.'

'Well no,' said Jim, 'but I put in a claim just in case they had, because we have been out of radio contact for three weeks, and it is very probable they will have incurred some damage.'

His favourite phrase, following such incidents, 'Anyway they owe us with their high premiums killing the trade.'

His financial acumen was admired from afar but the government was wary of his bonhomie and quick thinking. He certainly was an asset and managed to save the company considerable sums of money, particularly over custom land claims.

5

A Five Minute Strike

In Malaysia when you visited an estate's divisions you got into your Land Rover and off you drove. In the Solomons you climbed into your dugout canoe, powered by a 40 hp engine and off you sailed. For many of the divisions, or estates as they were called, were on islands which made up the Russells. Ufa was the closest and consisted of four islands. Further afield was the Pepesala group, while the southern estates on the main island were easier to reach by canoe than Land Rover. On every small coral island a few coconuts were growing, so in order to encourage the local Islanders to produce quality copra, we purchased most of the village crop as well, visiting their palm groves and making sure that the copra was dried to an acceptable standard.

*****

The seas were crystal clear, I sat in the bow to miss the spray and foam while the driver, mine was named Lascelles, sat in the stern and took the full force of the waves and spume as we ploughed into the troughs.

The canoes were hollowed out tree trunks, pointed in the bow. Fibreglass canoes were now being purchased by Islanders, although we continued to use wooden canoes which were considered more stable and seaworthy in rough seas and open water.

Needless to say all the canoe drivers were expert in their handling and never complained at the soaking they received nor the long hours they had to work. Lascelles was dependable and during the three years we lived in the Russells, never once did the outboard engine fail.

However he did have a propensity to sleep heavily once he had put me ashore. Having made the canoe safe he would lie down under the palms which fringed the islands and fall fast asleep, like all the drivers. At Pepesala, after a visit, I returned to the canoe with the Manager, Davidson Fekau, to find Lascelles absent. We called, to no avail, we sent a worker to scout for him. He was not to be seen, so I got into the canoe, lowered the engine and roared off into the lagoon and back to the main island. The sea was calm, I bypassed shallow shoals of coral, and remembered where there was deep water and emerging reefs, which necessitated slowing down, before entering deeper water where I was able to accelerate and plunge forward. Fortunately I remembered the channels and the jagged reefs below.

Dolphins played alongside the canoe, following as I skimmed along. Then, in the distance, the wharf at Yandina, which I reached at a pace of knots, skidding to a slurping halt at the jetty.

'Where is Lascelles?' the other boat drivers asked. 'Hey masta where him fella Lascelles go about?'

I replied, I didn't know, he must have gone walk about. They all looked surprised. 'He will come back on a barge,' they all agreed.

Evening came and went but there was still no sign of him. In the morning I drove down to the office, there was still no Lascelles, who would often come up to find out if I was travelling anywhere by canoe, but as I was going nowhere urgent I wandered over to the factory. Ron H. was in an amiable mood and we chatted about repair costs and the lack of trained artisans except for the Fijians and Samoans who had received excellent vocational training while attending apprenticeship courses on their native homeland islands.

By mid afternoon I was slightly concerned as to the whereabouts of my driver. Then, while working in my office, the door opened and in marched my erstwhile canoe driver.

'Me strike,' said Lascelles. 'You leave me behind, me go fishing,

Visiting the estates by canoe

you go, me strike.'

'Oh alright you strike, me get new driver for canoe belong me and you go cut copra.'

Silence, a puzzled frown slowly drifted over his face; he stood, scratched his nose, 'Me strike this minute now,' he repeated fervently.

'Yes, that's good one alright, myself likem plenty driving canoe, so me drive now, you findem job in field.'

'Ok, me strike over, strike him finish now, I go back along canoe.' Lascelles left my office happy with himself and his forceful action.

The fastest strike action ever was over in five minutes flat. I wish all labour relations difficulties could be solved as quickly as this boat-handling episode had been.

*****

Lever's operations completely revolved around sea travel and transport. Every day lighters pulled by small tugboat launches went out to the different islands to bring in the copra. All stores were transported in the same way, as well as tractors, bulldozers and other large pieces of equipment.

Copra as far away as Three Sisters was transported by landing craft. Likewise the copra from Kolambangara in the north. Cattle were transported to Honiara and from the Levers' ranch at Lunga. Only on the island of Yandina were Land Rovers used by myself, Jim and Ron Hutt and the cattle manager, Goodfella Fekau. This was necessary as the island had been divided up into four estates, a total of 12,000 acres, and the copra was tractor transported to feed the diesel powered copra dryers in the factory.

Moreover the economics of using sea transport over tractor-wheeled vehicles weighed heavily in favour of the sea, and from the distant corners of the main island, barges, wherever possible, were used in preference to wheeled transport.

There were disadvantages in sea travel, for human error, such as experienced with the Bank ship's calamity, could cause loss of boat and copra.

*****

One lunchtime Julia and I, while sitting by the shore under the shade of palms and a flame tree, watched with horror as a potential sea drama unfolded.

In the distance, midway between Ufa and the main island, a tugboat and four barges stacked with copra steamed homeward to unload their cargo. We watched and sipped our lime juice.

'What's happening?' asked Julia. 'What's that tugboat doing?'

I looked but saw nothing untoward.

'Go and fetch the binoculars,' ordered Julia.

I went inside the house got the binoculars and focused on the shipping. The barges were floating gently with the tide, but where was the tugboat? It was nowhere to the seen. I swept the seas and far in the distance noticed the tugboat by a reef.

'What the hell is it doing?' I asked. 'Has its engine stopped?'

No, the boat appeared to be moving. Far to its starboard the lighters slowly drifted onward. The sea was quite choppy and we noticed the lighters lurching heavily in the swell. I ran into the house to telephone the harbour superintendent. No answer. I telephoned Ron Hutt, but he was out with his mechanics repairing a water pump. I got into my Land Rover and rushed to the wharf. There was not a single canoe around; all the boats were out, not even Lascelles was in dock. The harbour was empty. Just then the harbourmaster arrived. I told him what was happening. He appeared unfazed. I asked him who was the Captain of the tug and was told it was Willie Catchem.

'Why has he dropped the barge lines?' I asked. Apprehension clouded Andifekau's face.

'Well?' I asked, 'You are in charge of sea transport.'

No answer.

A slightly embarrassed silence, again I repeated the question; what the hell was Willie doing?

'He's gone fishing,' came the reply.

'Fishing?' I exploded, 'He's fishing?'

'Yes sir, Willie often drops the lines and goes fishing when the sea is right.'

I took a deep breath, 'Send Willie to my office when he comes back,' I ordered, and then got into my Land Rover and drove home.

Julia was in a state of some excitement, because she also had now realised why the barges and the tugboat had dropped their umbilical cords.

'They've gone fishing,' she cried, as I came walking quickly to the shore where she was still sitting. 'I think they have caught something big. I will go to market when they come in.'

I looked at her coldly. 'You obviously find it exciting but that is a company ship and it's supposed not to be fishing.'

'Oh don't be so stuffy,' she replied, 'they are excellent seamen and know the reefs.'

I refrained from further comment.

In my office later there was a tap on the door and in walked Willie and Andifekau.

'What were you doing out there?' I demanded to know.

'Fishing,' replied Willie.

'Do you always go fishing?' I asked.

'Oh yes, when the sea is right.'

'Don't,' I said, 'do not ever drop your lighter's towlines again and go fishing. Fish from the tug but don't drop the lines.'

He looked disconcerted. 'Then how do we supply the market with fish?' he asked, 'all big fella missus buy fresh fish along market when I come back with copra,' he explained. 'Your missus she come along too.'

'No dropping lines again,' I said. 'Fish but no dropping lines or you will be cutting copra instead of being big fella Captain.' Willie well knew the value of his salary and perks.

'Right boss, fishing him stop finish.'

A few weeks later I asked Julia whether or not the fish on sale had declined in quantity. 'No, I don't think so', she answered, for she had heard that Lascelles and some of the canoe drivers were fishing far more than before when going to the islands.

'But Lascelles is with me,' I said.

'Oh yes but probably when you are on the estates he is catching fish and then leaving it for one of the tugboats to bring back with the copra.'

I never asked Lascelles if this was the case. It probably was, but at least the tugboats were not dropping their lines to go fishing.

*****

However it was not just the Bank Line that gave us problems. Having smashed our wharf, they decided not to come to the Russells until a new wharf had been built and declared fit for use. That meant another shipping line had to be sought to transport out our copra.

As our copra was mostly sold and shipped through the Solomon Island Copra Board of Honiara we asked them to search around for other ships willing to come to Yandina.

It was difficult, everybody knew of the Bank Line incident. Ships' captains were reluctant to navigate these difficult waters of dangerous reefs and narrow shoals. Cargo insurance premiums would have to be increased.

We were getting desperate, the godowns were full.

'We've got to get rid of the copra,' Ron Hutt cajoled us, 'now,' he said, 'we are full.'

At last the Copra Board found a steamer.

'We don't know its pedigree, but they are in the Solomons now, we will tell them to pick up the 500 tons already sold.'

We waited eagerly for their arrival. Then out of the mist one early morning, a vessel steamed in sweeping past our harbour, with the Captain on the bridge chart in hand.

Ron H. looked stunned. 'What is that?' he mumbled, for the ship looked in an exceedingly poor state of repair.

Having reached the end of the lagoon, it slowly retraced its steps.

We had rigged up a temporary pontoon jetty and waited with bated breath as the ship approached. However we need not have worried, the Captain was in command and the ship docked quietly without mishap.

The Captain was Finnish, young, but experienced. His crew were from the Philippines, with a Chinese engineer from Singapore. We quickly observed there was considerable friction between the Captain and the Engineer, which came to a head when the engineer abruptly entered our offices and asked for an airplane ticket back to Singapore.

31

'Don't be ridiculous,' I said, 'ask your Captain, not us.'

'He has no money,' said the engineer, 'and I am very sick with malaria. I haven't been paid, I want to leave now.'

'Well you can't,' I said. 'Get the ship loaded and off you go.'

We loaded the ship as quickly as possible. The Captain did not appear at all concerned with his recalcitrant crewmember.

'He's always like this,' he said, 'always complaining.'

'Perhaps because you haven't paid him,' we commented.

'No money,' he replied. 'The owners are very mean people. All Arabs, very mean. All money is finished.'

Loading was awkward and slow, too many nooks and crannies in the hold. The ships cranes were also out of action, all the bags of copra had to be manhandled aboard. Hot and sweaty work.

At last the 500 tons were on board.

'Off you go then, have a good voyage,' said Ron, after signing the various documents.

'The First Engineer is very sick,' came the reply from the Second Engineer.

'Well, the sooner you set sail then the better. Anyway, his malaria has gone so there is no other reason to hang around.'

We called the Captain.

'Safe journey,' I said. 'We need the jetty free, two coastal steamers are coming tomorrow.'

'The Engineer won't start up the engines,' the Captain groaned.

'Then get the Second Engineer to start up the bloody engines!' shouted Jim. 'He won't,' responded the Captain 'not without the First Engineer's permission.' 'If you don't move out in the next couple of hours we will tow you out,' I said. 'That's not allowed,' said the Captain, 'it is against maritime law.'

'We have only Lever's law around here, get those engines started or our landing craft and tugs will tow you away.'

The Captain returned to his ship.

We waited.

'Do we tow him off?' I was asked.

'Absolutely yes; when there is a fit, sick-free crew who will not go to sea without a valid reason, they are trespassing in our water, then other measures need to be taken. Anyway it's called mutiny.' I hoped I was correct with my facts.

Two hours elapsed; the ship lay quiet at the jetty. We drove down to the wharf, the Captain looked concerned.

'Are you going?' I asked.

'I can't,' he said.

We went on board; the engineer was on his bunk. I went up to him.

'You either leave now or we will tow you out to sea.'

He appeared not to believe me and shrugged his shoulders insolently and lay down on his cot. We left him, the Captain looked worried.

'Shoot the bugger, he is being mutinous,' said Jim.

Ron was already making the towing hawsers secure and a team of our wharfees were on board, very much enjoying the fun.

'Him big fellah Captain in for big surprise,' they chortled.

Kerosene Jim, who had also been supervising a loading gang, was making sure all the hatches were battened down, chuckling to himself, praying that he would be picked to stay on board to help, and also to see what happened next.

The Captain blanched.

'We will pull you to safe waters, then it is up to you.'

The Captain now appeared resigned to us carrying out our threat, and agreed to take the ship's helm.

Ron H. was in his element and took command from the landing craft's bridge. The hawsers tightened, Jim and I jumped ashore, the boat slowly left the jetty, the Captain on the bridge.

Immediately the ship's crew realized that this was a situation they had not reckoned with. Even the First Engineer now appeared on the bridge as Ron H. dutifully towed out the vessel. Throughout the ship the crew became galvanized by our precipitous action. Lounging seamen suddenly realizing that they also were part of the drama rushed to their posts as if carrying out emergency drill. Some just appeared mesmerized by the lapping sea upon the hull, leaning over and peering below as if seeking divine inspiration. The Captain on the bridge shouted commands, would the crew respond?

Further and further Ron pulled the vessel away; still there was no sound of engines being cranked into life. 'Oh dear, we thought, surely they must realize they have to do something. What happens if they get swept onto the reefs?'

Jim and I rushed back to my house, a better vantage point, to view the next episode of the drama.

'Oh look,' said Julia, with binoculars glued to her eyes, 'Ron is letting go the lines. I hope the ship doesn't run aground, I suppose you know what you are doing?' she queried, 'I am sure my father would not approve.'

'Possibly not,' I answered, 'but he doesn't happen to be here and we are and we don't want that ship lingering around anymore. It's in the way. Anyway,' coining the phrase of the moment, 'you can shoot mutineers, you know.' I said, nodding sagely at the same time.

'Not in 1978 you can't,' retorted Julia, 'that really would not go down at all well.'

I refrained from saying that her father, being an ex-naval officer, might well have approved and that her grandfather, a past Admiral, would have been positively delighted.

'Engines are firing!' shouted Jim excitedly. At last a thud of engines was heard, and slowly but surely the vessel with 500 tons of our copra onboard steamed away from the Russells, past the outer islands and reefs and headed out to sea, never to be seen again, by us.

6

Washing By The River

On land there were fewer mishaps, probably due to their being hardly any roads. Sea and air travel were the accepted, and often only, modes of transport.

On Guadalcanal a rough dirt road had been laid along a north-south axis. Around Honiara it was tarmaced and as far as the airport. After that the road was generally in a poor state of repair, especially during peak rains.

To reach our northern estate at Ruavatu, we drove. I usually borrowed a Suzuki 4 x 4, which was small, light and economical. It also, as Julia and I found out on one excursion to the estate, did not leak water when submerged and its engine appeared waterproof.

*****

On that occasion we left early morning, as usual, in order to try to get to the estate by early afternoon. We drove north past CDC's estates, through dry scrubland, past heavy infestations of the grass lalang (Imperatus cylindrica), the consequence of deforestation, beside pretty bamboo constructed villages with leaf thatched roofs, light and airy, and on to the River Baro.

The river was beautifully clear, unpolluted, swift and not too deep to be unfordable.

'Where is the ford?' I asked a villager standing on the riverbank.

He pointed to track marks going down into the river.

'Him ford,' he shouted back. I drove down into the water.

'It looks deep,' questioned Julia, 'are you sure this is the right place?'

I could feel the water pushing the vehicle sideways as we struggled on.

The water suddenly became deeper and deeper, I stopped the vehicle, the water lapped over the bonnet.

'Better climb out.' I told Julia. She opened her window fully and scrambled onto the roof, I joined her.

Parties of villagers began to arrive and found our predicament mildly amusing. Pipes were pulled out by both sexes as they deliberated upon this unusual event and then hunkered down to view.

'You followem wrong road,' was one cheerful cry.

'I know.' I said, 'Can you lift me out?'

They waded through the water towards us.

'Missus, she come along bank side now,' they said. So Julia, with water up to her bosoms and with the help of strong arms, slowly waded back to the riverbank.

A crowd of villagers were now squatting by the riverside to watch the next episode. Betel nut was chewed and spat out, pipes smoked and a pleasant carnival atmosphere blossomed as the sun arched higher in the sky.

However, the Suzuki did not budge. It was wedged firmly. We steadied ourselves around the vehicle. 'What now?' I wondered. Just then a police lorry arrived at the bank further downstream and out jumped a gang of prisoners guarded by a single unarmed jailor. It was all very relaxed, for they had come to do their weekly clothes washing.

I sloshed my way out of the river and walked down to the prisoners.

'Car belong me stuck too much, can I take your truck and findem tractor at CDC?' I asked the jailor.

Just then one of the prisoners called out, 'Hey him big fella belong Lever's, he put me in jail.'

Everybody stopped washing their clothes, the villagers shifted their gaze from the Suzuki back to me.

'Oh dear,' I thought, 'an unwanted intervention.'

Fortunately, as a prison sentence does not hold the same kind of stigma as it does in the West, or used to, nobody felt that this

Julia and the convicts

observation was particularly pertinent. Only in so much that 'big fella belong Levers' was in plenty trouble. And, it was certainly not going to dampen their afternoon's entertainment.

The jailor agreed to my request and I hopped into the lorry.

'What about me?' came a plaintive voice.

'Oh, hello, yes.' I had quite forgotten about Julia. 'I won't be long,' I called out, 'you will be quite safe with these thieves and rogues, they will look after you', I reassured her, smiling, giving her confidence.

'Hey,' I shouted to the prisoner, who I had supposedly imprisoned, 'you look good missus belong me, him bubbly (pregnant) too much.'

There was a murmur of interest from the assembled crowd now absorbed as the drama took another turn. More pipes were lit and puffed happily, while betel nut and tobacco were distributed on the ground in equal measure.

'Yes masta me lookem missus, me savvy too much missus gone bubbly.' This brought about further murmured sympathetic whisperings.

'Well thanks very much,' said Julia 'you are being incredibly thoughtful. This is just the kind of company I would choose as I enter the latter stages of pregnancy. Seven months, you know.'

'I won't be long,' I shouted back, 'they will look after you.'

*****

Indeed, having requisitioned a driver, a tractor and chain from the estate, it was not long before I was back, and for Julia time had passed equally quickly and by the time I arrived at the river she had learnt the life histories of most of those 'hardened criminals' while she sat amongst them commiserating over their misdemeanours. Once the Suzuki had been pulled out onto the Honiara side of the bank, we decided to return to Lunga estate for the night. The Suzuki fired first time, which was a relief, and we returned the same way as we had come.

'They seemed very nice criminals,' I said.

'Oh, not bad, however the nicest one was in for life, multiple murders apparently,' she said.

'Well cannibalism is no longer practised, so I am sure you were quite safe.' 'What from?' queried Julia, 'murder or cannibalism?'

'Well both,' I said, 'once you are dead, it doesn't really matter if you are gobbled up or not.'

There was silence.

'I suppose not, but I really would prefer to be buried properly in a graveyard than cooked in a pit with hot stones placed upon my belly,' replied a subdued Julia, 'and do drive slowly, he or she is kicking in hope of an early release.'

7

Flying In The Solomon Islands

It was extraordinary how well the Solomon Islands Airline managed to operate in the most difficult and severe weather conditions that the Pacific had to offer. Mountainous build-ups of cumulus-nimbus cloud would be jocularly pushed aside by the pilots as being there but 'no worries, we will fly around', or 'we will find a gap', or 'it's a biggun, lets have a dash at getting through'.

Some of the pilots did not have many hours, far fewer than I had, hoping to log up as many as possible before returning to Aussie to apply for a job with Quantas or Ansett. That is if they had not applied before and been turned down. Many were just not sufficiently competent to fly for a major airline.

I flew frequently, as a passenger, to Lever's outer island properties and became acquainted with some of the longer serving pilots. Although too often, when one asked 'Where's Jack today?' the reply would be, 'Oh yeah he's gone back to Aussie. Pity, good man, fair dinkum pilot too.' This sentiment was usually expressed as you sat huddled in your seat with a backdrop of massive cumulus, mingled with a slatey curtain of rain moving inexorably in your direction.

'And when did you come?' I then asked

'Oh last week, just getting a feel of flying the islands, it's certainly different from Aussie.'

'Yes, well, do please try avoiding the mountains to your left,' I usually had to remind them when returning to Yandina from Honiara, 'they are actually 6,000 feet and we are at 4,500 feet.'

'Oh yeah, thanks for telling,' comes back the polite response, then a mild laugh, 'I want to get back to Honiara tonight there's a piss up at the Yachtie (Yacht Club). Last night got so boozed I couldn't recognize me missus.'

'Oh,' I said, surprised, 'I thought all you pilots left your wives behind or were unmarried or divorced.'

'Yeah that's right,' came back the reply; a snuffled chortle followed this priceless piece of eloquence, 'that's why I didn't recognize me wife.'

The resultant guffaw usually awoke the trembling passengers. However they were always pleased when a pilot with a happy disposition was in command. Whether or not he was a good pilot was immaterial; a good sort, plenty of laughs bred confidence.

*****

Taking off or landing on the islands was seldom hazardous as many of the runways had been built for American war planes during World War II and therefore were long and well-surfaced.

However once in the air the whole scenario changed, particularly during the afternoon when the cumulus thickened and huge cavernous mountains of cloud, like steepling naves of a cathedral, reared inwards to overhang the small planes as they battled through the evening dusk and turbulence; it appeared as if a massive witch was threatening to strike the planes down.

Most pilots tried to avoid the cloud, those inexperienced drove straight through the middle because they did not know better, or, had left their detour too late.

'What do we do now mate?' my favourite pilot, Bill, asked, during one exceptionally awful flight from Kolambangara. 'Do we go back, find a way through or go down below?'

'If we go down we will hit the sea, we are now too far in,' I reply. 'Look for a break we could be lucky.'

We climb further into the witches' cauldron of blackness. There were only three other passengers aboard, none were enjoying this flight one little bit.

Rain beat down, the plane rocked, visibility was a few metres. Bill concentrated on his instruments while rivulets of sweat slid down his face dampening his shirt. My heart leapt high as the plane fought for air, captured by another empty air pocket.

He was likeable, but whenever I happened to be in the Solomon Islands (S.I) Civil Aviation Department office for some reason or other, Bill would also be there, either taking an exam or awaiting a result, or being chastised or, just seemingly passing the time of day with an irate official. Always looking harassed and probably wishing he was somewhere else, preferably driving a bus in Sydney.

I liked him, he was not the best pilot around, but he tried hard, was diligent and remarkably civilised, his passions were art and music, principally classical. He suddenly lets out a snort, 'Look!' he says. Amidst the blacks and greys and sluicing rain, there is a glimmer at the end of the tunnel. A brief smile heralds the news. He concentrates and flies straight for the light. We slice through into a magnificent lingering evening glow. There are huge sighs of relief from behind; the smell is acrid but very human.

Bill looks happier now.

'We are running out of light,' he mutters.

'You had better stay at Yandina, don't go on tonight or you might be grounded. Anyway you are not allowed to fly after dark are you?' I query.

'No that's right but I want to get back to meet my piccaninny sheila.'

'Well I wouldn't, it's too late now.'

*****

We land at Yandina and he comes back to the house for a feed and then goes onto the Company rest house to kip down for the night.

Bill did not last long, he had had enough of flying in the islands and probably the islands had had enough of Bill. He sought a calmer life and became an interior house decorator in Brisbane, allowing him time to indulge in his painting.

8

Rebecca

Rebecca was born on the 8th day of August in 1978, 30 years ago today. Rather than be subjected to the torment of the S. I. Medical services of Honiara, Julia returned to the more pleasant and hygienic atmosphere of the Penzance Bolitho Nursing Home, with a view out to sea and the Penzance Newlyn Rugby Club to the rear.

It was a sensible decision because for the expatriate community the lack of good medical treatment was becoming intolerable. There were sufficient doctors, but their sole aim was to tend to the needs of the native community. This was expected, but not to the complete exclusion of the numerous expatriates that lived, worked and governed the Islands.

'Try Brisbane,' they said, 'we are too busy here.'

'You should be open to all members of the public, we pay taxes, part of your wages, the health service is for us as well', we complained.

Lever's personnel had always relied upon the island's medical services before, the position now needed to be reviewed.

Julia, during her pregnancy had to wait hours to see a doctor, who was generally officious, uncaring and disinterested.

'I am the wrong colour,' Julia would say after another harassed visit to the clinic.

Jim was equally angry, 'No more freebies for the doctors when they visit Lever's properties, we'll clean up our hospital and take on medical staff which will serve the plantations and the outer islands. We will break even,' he drawled.

So back to the UK went Julia, thankful that she would not be attended to by a doctor who treated malaria patients with aspirin and thought syphilis was yaws.

Rebecca's arrival into the world was swift and simple. Julia returned to the islands with this very lively creature who started to run at six months and would be taken daily to the factory where she played on the heaps of dried cocoa beans, nibbled the drying copra as it was bagged and was allowed to play up and down the elevators when idle.

*****

Our lives, except for the medical situation, were idyllic. On most Sundays we took a picnic and, with Lascelles driving, canoed out to the many small outer islands that fringed the Russells and which provided a bulwark to the endless battering of the Pacific.

There we swam, snorkelled, read and lounged about under the coconut palms and jungle trees that fringed the shore. Lascelles went fishing, Jim and Peggy often came out and we would be joined by any visitor who happened to be staying at Yandina.

Julia started a small collection of the many different shells which could be found on the coral shore, in the small lagoons, often buried close to the beche-de-mer, which abounded in those seas. The Islands were considered to harbour the greatest concentration of cowrie shells in the world and collectors from all four corners would come to seek out the rarest and in the Russells the richest and most diverse assembly of shells were to be found.

Snorkelling gave us great pleasure and we would swim over the precipitous coral shelf into a void of blue, streaked by the pale sparkling light of the sun which filtered downward. Floating as if in space, a sensation of languid falling, an Indian dance in the sea, arms and body moving graceful, uninhibited and limbless, through azure blues and darting brilliantly coloured coral fish. It was bliss.

Meanwhile Rebecca gurgled and floated her way along the shore, oblivious of the myriad fish which joined her and below, the predators, the sharks and barracuda, jostled together in the deep waters a few metres away.

Sharks of all shapes and sizes, small reef sharks, black tipped, white and grey tipped, the killers, hammerhead and tiger, intense and purposeful, endlessly moving, always inquisitive and possibly wondering what tribe this little splodge of humanity belonged to as she boldly floated above.

*****

Julia and I found the shark population intimidating, especially once when snorkelling off Pepesula we were confronted by a tiger shark. Fortunately we were swimming in shallow water so his aggressive movement towards us was hindered by the jagged coral outcrops we were snorkelling amongst. Others, particularly the professional divers and the marine biologists who frequented the Solomons, would treat the sharks with respect and distain in equal measure; the reef sharks predating amidst the island's coral cladding were often merely regarded as irritants.

One such couple, Debbie and Jim Prescott, both marine biologists who lived on the Russells, appeared to have no fear. Once when I was driving their canoe while waiting for them to surface, Debbie emerged with a snapping school of reef sharks biting at her flippers.

'Hi,' she called, 'how are you?' as polite Americans do.

She came alongside, got another roll of film or whatever, and submerged in a bubble of frenzied fins, totally unconcerned, quite oblivious to the agitation her presence had caused.

Others were of the same fearless mould. Brian Bailey, a professional diver living in Honiara, was on one occasion propelled backwards by a tiger shark he had been keeping at bay with his spear gun. Not wishing to fire the gun, which would have immediately attracted other patrolling sharks eager to grab a portion of their dying comrade and probably a piece of Brian as well, he abandoned his gun and shot to the surface. Fortunately his waiting canoe was close by and Brian was able to quickly scramble aboard before his finned adversary realised that it had just missed a meal of succulent Aussie prime thigh. Angrily the shark torpedoed to the surface and brushed against the canoe trying to dislodge its inhabitants and then departed the scene in a threshing huff.

Such experiences were commonplace, but definitely not for Julia or me. We were quite content with the serene beauty of the lagoons, the tiny bays, sandy shores and the exquisitely decorated coral; we experienced this scene daily, it never palled.

The ever present sharks did not inhibit our sailing activities. We bought from the U.K. a fibreglass boat, a Sailfish, with a single mast, a small well to sit in and dagger keel. It went like the wind and we often packed our afternoon tea into a haversack, tied it to the mast and with Julia clutching onto to Rebecca, precariously, sped across the waters to Talina Island, one of the Ufa group.

Here we enjoyed the peace of a secluded shady inlet where nothing disturbed the tranquillity of the gentle afternoon warmth, then to return home across the sea as the sun began to dip behind the horizon.

9

Yachts and Visitors

Our deep-water lagoon was a haven for yachts. They sailed in on their way to and from other ends of the Pacific and their presence was a welcome relief at Yandina.

They also came to stock up on meat, for our butchery provided a whole range of delicious cuts. Each Friday steers were slaughtered and hung for the following week, and all of us lived on the most delicious steak and fish. Lascelles also frequently collected huge oysters for us from the mangroves or off the wharf pilings. Surprisingly, vegetables were a luxury as no Islander had mastered the art of growing them competently.

A ferro-cement junk, built in Hong Kong, was a regular visitor. The owners had circumnavigated the Pacific for the past ten years. It was a splendid vessel, with all mod cons and, a vegetable garden on board. Tomatoes, chillies, green pepper, planted in pots, adorned the stern and provided fresh vegetables whilst at sea.

The owners, Joe and Elena, were Americans and had made a lot of money by inventing a barbecue oil. They then decided to take off, leave civilisation behind, and roam the seas. At each school holiday their children joined them, flying to the nearest airport to where they were anchored.

They were a happy and contented couple and would stay at Yandina for weeks on end, enjoying the island and calm harbourage. Julia, Rebecca and I often went on board in the evening. It was blissful but also somnolent and the inactivity would, for us, have been oppressive. They, however, were writing a book of their adventures and the marine life they had observed and studied during their voyages.

Both were highly experienced divers and would often explore the wrecks of the many Japanese battleships which had been sunk off the Islands during World War II. After one exploration feat they brought back two sake cups retrieved from a sunken ship's wardroom. These were given to Rebecca as a christening present.

Another frequent visitor was a leg-less mariner, a fine example of what a disabled person could manage. His yacht was equipped in such a fashion that he never had to move and could carry out every activity with his arms and hands, which were indeed well-muscled. He was more than content sailing the seas on his own.

*****

Government officials occasionally came for the day and left in the evening. As the government owned a share of the company and the permanent secretary to the Minister of Agriculture sat on the board, their visits were never pleasing, but usually they only came over, at government expense, for the meat, the fish, and a pleasant afternoon of beer sliding down thirsty gullets at the Lever's club on Yandina. Most were pleasant, left of centre, not very hardworking, but genuinely loved the Solomons. They were often married to local ladies, and after Independence had no intention of leaving.

While on the other side of two oceans Unilever remained extremely concerned as to whether or not Levers S. I. had a viable future and company directors, engineers, agronomists and others periodically put in an appearance to assess the scene, fortunately, owing to difficult plane connections and, of course, distances, the number of visits were always limited to the bare necessity.

10

The Hybrid Coconut Palm

Company Directors sought to economise whenever possible. For management on the plantations the most important aspects to consider were costs, production and crop husbandry.

Economizing meant cutting costs. Improved production usually implied an increase in volume, higher expenditure but lower unit costs. Sometimes it was difficult to marry the two conflicting differences of opinions, downsizing versus upsizing.

Now that the company was planting hybrid coconuts, the progeny derived from coupling female flowers of dwarf palms with male pollen from selected tall palms, it was hoped that yields from the resultant progeny would rise. The price of coconut oil was buoyant and the World Bank's projected figures were encouraging; of the vegetable oils sluicing around the world, coconut oil appeared to be one of the most desirable.

Historically the coconut was regarded only as an essential ingredient of the peasant farmer's backyard cropping system rather than as a commodity crop of commercial potential. A very useful tree, but assigned to the rear of the house beside the drop pit toilet, where it flourished.

It was Mr. Lever who promoted the coconut as an industrial crop, to be established on plantations rather than in backyards, and which would produce sufficient oil for his soap factories. In consequence coconut plantations began to become established during the 1920s and 1930s.

*****

However, oil palms were also being planted throughout Asia in ever increasing quantities. The processed tonnage of crude palm oil (CPO) from one hectare was four times that of coconuts. Coconuts could become economically unviable, for palm oil was now the cheapest oil on the world stage.

Something had to be done. Coconut oil yields had to increase for the plantations to survive. The palms needed to be more competitive, although oil palms if introduced would not have thrived on the Island's coral sands. However all was not lost for, far away in the Ivory Coast, IRHO, the French Research Institute on Oils, was venturing into improving coconut yields through adopting a programme of hybridisation.

At the same time Unilever's research establishment also had become involved in production improvement and the first commercial plantings of hybrids at Yandina were planted in 1973. They grew and were considered a success. Thereafter it was decided all future replantings would use hybrid planting material.

Company expenditure rose as more hybrids were planted. Firstly on Somata Island of Pepesala group and then on Ufa. Jim's financial calculations looked ominous. Production from the hybrids would be almost double that of a local tall palm, but fertilizer expenditure and manpower costs would also be heavy. Increased wage rates were also being scrutinized by the government as Independence drew closer. Would the hybrid be economically viable?

Calls of anguish from London, once muted, became more strident and frequent. Improved productivity was essential.

Fortunately cocoa prices were still rising. The coconut oil market remained buoyant, but overall plantation costs were increasing as the old palms were removed and hybrids planted.

'Stop planting,' Jim suggested.

'Can't,' I cried, 'we have seed gardens operating non-stop, our nurseries have tens of thousands of seedlings, what's happened to the budget?'

Would the hybrids make a significant difference? The experts were positive. Certainly French results were bullish, but managing commercial plantings was not the same as looking after small research demonstration plots. And why was there so much secrecy surrounding Palawan Island in the Philippines where huge hybrid seed gardens had been established? Other than a few government officials and French research personnel nobody was allowed to enter the complex.

French research and expertise, possibly not conclusive, was still in its infancy, Unilever's also. Perhaps hybrid coconuts were not going to perform to expectations, but they had, we were told, in the Ivory Coast, and in the Philippines thousands of hectares were being established with hybrid planting material. But now reports coming out indicated otherwise.

Zamboanga (Mindanao), the main coconut-growing region of the Philippines, in truth had hardly planted a hybrid seednut; it was a sham. Big deals had been perpetrated. Hybrid planting material had been sent across oceans from the Ivory Coast to Mindanao and also from Palawan, the bright hope of future seed garden production.

Meanwhile we continued planting, using seednuts harvested from our own seed gardens, meticulously pollinated, collected and germinated in our own nurseries and then replanted in the old desiccated senile palm groves. Research officers came and viewed. All were bullish. Jim wasn't and I now was beginning to have doubts, especially as news percolated through that tending hybrid plantings was an expensive operation. The French visited and left extolling the virtues of the hybrid. They would, they had invented it, but with the French the elan goes into the concept, which has to be supported at all costs whether the end result is satisfactory or not. To admit failure is not in their language.

11

Independence 1978

Amidst all our commercial concerns, Independence Day drew nearer. A committee was formed to organise the celebrations. School children would run races; there would be a tug of war, the perennial favourite, a copra cutting competition, horsemanship, seven-a-side rugby and a whole host of other events were scheduled for the day.

The Duke of Gloucester was to hand over the reins to the new Governor in Honiara. All was prepared throughout the Islands and Yandina was going to celebrate in style. A New Zealand Air Force plane was to provide a solo fly past and a Royal Naval frigate would steam past as the new Solomon Island flag was raised and the Union Jack lowered.

But where was the new flag? Everybody hunted high and low. Had it arrived? The day was tomorrow. 'The police, they must have it, it can't be lost!' but indeed it was.

The Yandina rugby ground was prepared, the running lines marked, the horses groomed. Cattle were slaughtered; fires for cooking fringed the ground. A grandstand was erected and Julia was to present the prizes. The crowds arrived, workers, locals, outsiders and a few yachtsmen caught up in the carnival spirit. But still no flag.

'Can we stitch another as an interim measure?' asked the accountant's wife.

'It must be somewhere,' I groaned.

'Jim's house!' somebody yelled. Jim was representing Levers in Honiara.

Ron rushed off, there were only a few minutes to go before the celebrations started and the band played the new national anthem.

'Do we know the words?' I asked Julia.

'No I don't,' she replied.

'Well you should, you are the musician of the family.'

A policeman walked briskly over.

'We are ready,' he said.

The flag! Where was Ron?

At that moment a Land Rover hurtled to a standstill at the rear of the grandstand and our pink, perspiring engineer trotted through the dignitaries, with the new national emblem wrapped in a John Tom Stores brown paper bag.

All set, the band played, the flag was tied to the flagpole rope. Smart policemen saluted the flag as it climbed gently up the pole fluttering friskily in the breeze. Everybody applauded, then the Union Jack came down and was folded and handed to the officer-in-charge. The end of an era, all smiles, waves for the plane which dipped its wings and raucous shouts of glee greeted the frigate as it swept slowly by. 'Well-timed,' I thought, 'and now for the games'.

Every game was played with incredible enthusiasm under the hot midday sun. The cattlemen on their smartly groomed horses manoeuvred inelegantly around the field, Joe Lynn, our horse trainer, cringed. Julia said nothing. Applause all around.

By early evening most of the participants playing rugby were exhausted, as were the crowd. The seven-a-side final was between the Police and Yandina 'B', in which I had been included. I was nearing forty and seven-a-side rugby was tiring, one last burst was required. We scurried, made mighty tackles, of which only Pacific Islanders are capable and floated the ball to speedy wings.

Breathless, 'This is ridiculous,' I thought, 'my end is nigh'. We lose, smelly handshakes and pats, shirts exchanged. My opposite number takes off his shirt, I do in exchange. His body is massive, a ring of teeth incisions encircle his upper torso.

'What happened?' I ask.

'Oh me get half bitten by one big fellah shark,' came the reply. 'Me go fishing, him big fellah catch me here', and he points to the teeth marks, I stare. 'I loosem my fish too', he continued, 'him mighty big fellah, but I loosem.'

He appeared more upset about losing the fish than being almost bitten in half by a shark.

*****

Fireworks ended the day and a mountain of meat was consumed. Beer stubbies littered the ground, drunkenness claimed many. Julia and I retreated.

'This here Independence party, him plenty good spirit, we want another next year, him mighty good time, every one fellah him drunk. Next year we want day belong Independence this time again.'

These sentiments were expressed by one of the tractor drivers about to load his trailer full of reeling, well-fed workers, ready for an early kip and then more revelry later.

'This Independence thing could go on forever,' said Julia. 'I wonder if they realize what it is all supposed to mean.'

Next day was a holiday but on the following day, the company continued as normal. There was no perceptible difference between 100 years of days before and this day after.

'Solomon Islanders should understand that we are now all equal,' Julia remarked.

'I am not sure that would be good idea,' I dreamily surmised.

'Why not?' she retorted sharply, 'the islands have their own government now.' 'Yes, but without the companies there will be no more blissful peace. We keep the peace through employment and our taxes pay for the democracy that they are about to enjoy. A new Government is to be installed tomorrow.'

Independence was a very enjoyable non-event. Nothing changed, a parliament was voted in and a Solomon Islander replaced the Australian Governor as Head of State.

Before going on leave to the U.K. I called in at State House. The gate guards no longer appeared quite as crisp and eager as before. I wandered through, nobody was about, I called, no one answered. 'I wonder where the Governor is?' I asked myself. 'Probably in the snooker room'. I walked through the house to the snooker room; on the table lay the Governor fast asleep, benign, gently snoring. I scribbled a note and departed. Where else in the world could one walk into the Head of State's house unannounced and, in a scribbled memo left delicately on a heaving tummy, request their presence for drinks on the Mendana Terrace at 6.00 p.m.

12

We Leave The Solomons

A cattleman by trade and a rice agronomist by training, Jack Tounour, when on a mission to the Solomons for the Australian Development Assistance Bureau (ADAB), approached me concerning providing a tree crop input for a project being funded by ADAB in the Philippines.

The project was to be located in one of the poorest provinces of the Philippines, Samar, where most of the people were peasant farmers, catholic in belief and left wing in political and social aspirations. They were all very poor.

'Let's go,' said Julia, 'it will coincide with our leave. There is music in Manila and none here and good medical facilities too.'

She had recently suffered a miscarriage and was not pleased with the lack of medical assistance on offer.

'But you like it here don't you?' I asked.

It was now three years since we joined Lever's.

'Very much indeed, but there is a bamboo organ in Manila that I should like to play, plus two very good orchestras.'

She appeared to know rather a lot about the music scene in the capital and that couldn't have been gleaned from Jack, who although extremely nice, knew little of the arts and regarded the Sydney Racing News as the nearest thing to culture that he would ever read.

The thought of branching out into agricultural consultancy, now in its infancy, would be an interesting change for me.

We were going on leave. Perhaps my twenty years on plantations could be usefully employed in another theatre of agronomy.

Jim was unhappy, 'What the hell for?' he asked. 'It's a fantastic lifestyle. We are a great team; they hate us in government (pre Independence) which must be good. Julia what have you been doing to this guy?'

It was all said as friendly banter. But he was sad and within a couple of years Jim had also gone, entering the employ as financial advisor to one of the many rich Arab princes who inhabited the Gulf States.

Unilever's were very kind and my pension after three years of service was equivalent to over half that I received from H & C's after seventeen years. Julia, Rebecca and I returned to Penberth, planted some vines and then left for the Philippines. A new life as a consultant had begun.

13

A Muddle In Samar 1980

The project was a muddle, for the principal objective was to build a road from the west of the province starting at San Jose through to Catarman, the main provincial town of North Samar.

This provided a dilemma for the Labour government of Australia, for without doubt the road would be used to transport Filipino troops quickly to and from trouble spots whenever the peasants attempted an uprising, however minor. 'If we build this road, as the Philippine Government has requested,' it facilities army mobilization and that is not a policy we ought to support,' the Australians argued.

'On the other hand,' we reasoned, 'farmers and businesses will benefit, through easy movement of crops and services.'

The dilemma was deliberated upon at length. At our project head office on the outskirts of Manila, adjacent to a dog abattoir (Filipinos love dog meat which is regarded as a gourmet dish therefore strays are endlessly rounded up to satisfy demand), we pondered and discussed the issues at stake.

ADAB was providing assistance to build a road, which could be usefully employed by the local farmers, Jack and I argued.

'Who cares about the army? They are around whatever we do.'

'The farmers need plants,' I continued. 'Every farmer in the world knows how to plant a seed or seedling. Filipinos are versatile, they can bud, graft, layer, grow cuttings, sow seeds, propagate anything you name. They have a history of good plant husbandry. They, however, want access to good seed, plants, chemicals, fertilizer, a market, diversification, then they will take off and become more productive. They distrust authority and a road will help them communicate with the markets and be prosperous.'

I was not used to all this ridiculous fatuous deliberation on what a peasant needed. He knew he wanted seeds and sense and a market, but we seemed to be offering only words and systems.

I was being introduced to a new jargon, cooperation, integration, sustainability, bottoms up, top down; women in development (WID), institutional building and more and others and more. Perhaps this is what consultancy was all about, jargon and reports, never to be read, stockpiled in an office, forgotten.

What a waste of time and money.

Jack agreed. 'Let's get some hybrid coconuts from Palawan and go and plant them,' Jack suggested. 'We will need a few million there are a lot of peasants in the villages.'

Cries of anguish from the economist, 'You must mean hundreds, a demonstration plot only, we are not a supply depot we have to build the institution first to receive and look after the nuts.'

'They know how to look after nuts,' I retorted, 'the Philippines is the biggest supplier of coconut oil in the world. They have been planting coconuts since the year dot. What kind of institution is needed? Extension officers can open up nurseries along your lovely nonexistent new road. The villagers will germinate the seednuts and later plant the seedlings behind their non-flush toilets. They know already how to plant coconuts.'

Sour faces, what a bunch! Most had never seen a coconut seedling, coffee flowers were pretty, what was a paddy field? Practical knowledge - nil. Systems and institutions were well known and upon which the extension personnel and economists contented themselves in their desire to provide assistance. So easy, no fieldwork required, office lounging only and the never ending writing of reports and memos and, of course, seminars, uncountable, once a week or more.

There were always a dozen constraints to one opportunity. Whatever was suggested, those who were meant to benefit would not, while those doing the implementation would.

The Filipino institutions, operationally, appeared dysfunctional except they soaked up the unwanted semi-educated mass of inertia which existed throughout their society; providing assistance and advice to the farmers was beyond their capabilities. But it did not really matter. Farmers were capable, they learnt from their more progressive neighbours, from the surrounding estates and commercial enterprises. They communicated amongst themselves, listened to farming programmes on their radios, the BBC World Service's commodity price updates were followed daily. The Government's district agricultural offices housed bureaucrats, harbingers of gloom, ignorant and unpractical. Self-important and condescending, unreceptive to change. The farmers did not need them.

These were the institutions we were to assist. But what about the farmer Jack and I pleaded in vain for?

It was increasingly obvious that all the Filipinos really wanted was the road, the hardware and materials, any money sluicing around and, of course, please buy us lots of lovely hybrids.

*****

Jack and I went to Samar. There were a few moderately wealthy landlords who owned a lot of land, which should have been considerably more productive than was apparent. While the vast majority of the people were helplessly poor and undernourished, they were religious and the priests and nuns maintained a fierce grip upon their spiritual allegiance, but when it came to filling stomachs, socialist principles or the communist faith had the edge.

61

In the hills and jungle beyond Catarman the peasants eked out a subsistence living; a staple diet of rice and salt seldom varied. Young girls suckled babies, a woman of twenty-three years had already five children and lived in a shack, daily drawing water, cooking, cleaning, humping firewood. Then a year later another baby. Death often an early release from her drudgery.

Our typist Florence was the same, nineteen years old with three children. 'How many more?' I asked.

A shrug. 'My husband wants more.'

'Surely three is enough, you are beautiful you will soon lose your looks with all the children you have. And work. Your husband must also help.'

A sigh. 'God likes us to have children.'

'Yes he does,' I reply, 'but not so many that you cannot feed them.'

The Roman Catholic Church had much to answer for.

'Why don't you tell them to practise birth control, stop them from breeding?' I would entreat the nuns when stopping over for the night at a church rest house. They were kind and gentle but dogmatic and would argue fiercely and unswervingly in defence of their beliefs, to die for the Pope would be an honour.

'Birth control is not condoned,' they would reply.

'People are starving, there are millions of children out there to feed.'

'It is God's blessing,' came the reply.

'And so I presume is hunger, poverty and death,' I would retort.

It is impossible to argue against belief, for its all in the mind and such a fixation can seldom be unlocked. No different to the Muslim world of today, I thought.

Jack had the right approach.

'Why argue?' he said as we sat at a stall one evening dinking beer, it also served delicious slender barbecued chicken legs, 'you will never change a nun's mindset. They are noble but unwavering and however wrong you think the church's attitude is over birth control only the Pope has the power to change a doctrine and he won't because he is celibate, so therefore does not understand the iniquity of uncontrolled birth rates, and, sure as sure few will ever tell him.'

*****

I went to Palawan to purchase hybrid seednuts, but failed. Nobody would allow me to visit the seed gardens. It was guarded as if it housed a strategic missile base. I went to Zamboanga to try to buy some of the millions already sent there. Only rotting heaps were visible. I went to a land scheme where hybrids had been planted, they were suffering from a lack of fertilizer; it was too costly, I was told; yields were not up to expectation.

I wrote to Jim reciting my tale of woe.

'Told you so,' came back the reply.

Had I developed a fixation on hybrids; is it all a big mistake? I went to Los Banos the University of Philippines, close to Manila, and visited the Plant Breeding faculty where Mrs Gutzman, a coconut expert, was involved in a haphazard programme of tissue culture, product quality control and hybrids.

She was noncommittal, but suggested we planted a wide range of selected Philippine cultivars, the Catigan, the Tacunan, Laguna Tall and others. Although they were not hybrids yields were exceptional and would certainly over a lifetime out-perform any hybrid.

'Anyway this whole programme at Palawn is flawed,' she told me, 'all expertise, technology, management systems are imported, it is not a Filipino project there is a lot of money involved.'

I returned to Samar despondent.

*****

Jack was planting rice at the University of Catarman.

'We have to start somewhere,' he said. 'We must feed our Filipino support staff who cannot afford to buy sufficient rice and therefore need some food to keep them going.'

There were cries of outrage from the Australian extension officers and economists.

'We are not here to feed the people,' they said, 'we are here to rebuild their institutions so that they can feed themselves in the future.'

'There may not be a future at this rate,' replied Jack, 'there are a million hungry people out there.'

Meanwhile what was I doing? Well very little, I had picked up a couple of officers from the local governments' agricultural bureau; knowledgeable but disinterested and without ambition, for there was nothing in it for them and they were definitely not eager to travel away from Catarman.

Dangerous, they said; I could hardly blame them, they were poorly paid, lacked resources of any kind and each had to provide for a large dependent family.

I found the whole issue of aid dispiriting. We spent so much time talking ourselves out of doing anything. All negative, even the preparation work on the road seemed to have stalled. Another anguished purging of our plans was taking place.

So I packed my Toyota Land Cruiser and, with four armed guards, went in search of the truth. We journeyed east, over mud and sand, through swamp and forest, past the ubiquitous water buffalo preparing the paddy fields; stopping off asking questions, always the same answer, it was the Provincial Governor's fault. Self-help amongst the peasants was minimal except to plant sufficient crops to survive.

'Grow more,' I pleaded.

'What for?' they asked.

'Profit,' I said.

Too many mouths to feed, negative shaking of heads indicated their despair.

'Have fewer babies,' I implored.

This issue they could not contemplate.

'The church would never agree to birth control,' they whispered.

Everywhere I went an avalanche of children straggled their way home once school was over for the day. What hope was there for them in these over-populated and impoverished islands?

I cannot believe that God, up there, pointing to the ceiling of the nave of a church in the town of Nenito I was visiting, applauds and wishes these poor people to go on having more and more babies.

'He just wouldn't approve,' I argued with the priest. 'It is just not acceptable.'

'It is the will of the Lord,' came back the reply, as always.

'How possibly can you say that?' I counter. 'He is up there and you have control down here. It is your will not His.'

*****

I often stayed with the landlords. Many did not enjoy living in the rural areas. They regarded the peasants as being unmotivated, lazy, slothful and dishonest.

'Treat them better,' I would say, 'and they will become more productive.'

They approved of President Marcos and the imposed discipline. Which was to their advantage.

'Beware of communism,' they urged upon me.

'Do you know any communists?' I asked.

'Oh yes many,' was the frequent reply.

'Look,' said one, 'that boy outside there, he is a communist his parents are dead, shot by the army.'

'Well he certainly doesn't look very dangerous,' I reply.

'No he is not, we give him work and food. We pray daily for his conversion.'

A weekend away dealing with issues on their farms and then back to Manila for a good time. Possibly taking in a visit to the Manila Cultural Centre to listen to the Philharmonic Orchestra in which Julia is now ensconced as first clarinettist.

14

Manila and Music

What an extraordinary country is the Philippines. Mass poverty, extreme riches, both side by side. I returned to Manila every other week. Julia was happy playing in an orchestra at the Manila Cultural Centre and enthused over the 400 year old bamboo organ at Las Pinas Church, Manila. For her, Manila was a musical haven. For Rebecca less so, for she had reached the tender age of two and found playing in the Makati Park tame compared to swimming with sharks in the Russells. However she made up for her boredom through tantrums, which she displayed with unnerving frequency, usually in the most crowded of places.

Filipinos love children and would rally round Julia and our nanny in order to try and pacify Rebecca out of her tantrum. She was not to be appeased and screamed even louder, and only when ignored did she revert back to normal. Whatever that was.

*****

There seemed, after concerts, endless parties to go to. I was allowed to tag along as well. Mostly musicians and followers, everybody had to play something. One notable display of virtuosity, completely spontaneous, was performed by the conductor Red Romero and his first violinist when they took up their violins, while preparing food in the kitchen, and played the Bach double violin concert to great applause.

The Filipinos are so musical. Theirs is a great talent, they can play or sing anything, a wonderful gift which Julia in her experience had never come across before. They are so incredibly versatile, after only two rehearsals with the Sadlers Wells Ballet Company they can now play the whole ballet. Even the visiting conductor, Colin Metters, an ex-student friend of Julia's at London's Royal College of Music, was enthusiastically surprised.

*****

It was fun and entertaining, the music of the highest quality, and the parties afterwards exotic and exhilarating. But quite extraordinary for often the house or apartment where we gathered would be a mere street away from a fetid slum, where the inhabitants would be incarcerated behind reinforced concrete walls.

Yet people like Red Romero, Red because he was a self-confessed socialist or even worse, understood the extreme hardship and suffering that was common throughout the country's archipelago of a thousand islands. But they were powerless, as the dictatorship which governed was well supported by the Americans, whose attitude was that anything must be better than communism. It was anathema to the White House in Washington.

And the Philippines were completely enmeshed with everything American. One almost felt as though the country was joined by an umbilical cord to the other side of the Pacific. America's influence in the Philippines over the past eighty years had been completely dominant. However they had left a legacy of incompetence, the country's bureaucracy was poorly conceived and inadequately trained. The civil service and judiciary were non-existent. Compared to their neighbours Malaysia or Singapore, the country was an ungovernable mess.

It is a pity that the Philippines were not colonised by the British, I enthused, when periodically I became outraged with the ineffectiveness and casual indifference exhibited by the various authorities we were having to cooperate with.

It was true though, little happened without some form of

recompense. Corruption was rife throughout all layers of society; the millions of nobodies at the bottom of the social ladder hardly cared, except for themselves, understandably, while only those in the middle and at the top, who supported the incumbent oligarchy, enjoyed the benefits that a dictatorship had to offer.

15

A Year of Nil Achievement and Hope

'I am just as bad as everybody else,' I think to myself. 'I have been here a year, my contract is for one year, but renewable, and I have done very little, achieved nothing of importance, learnt the new jargon, so therefore I am now equipped to enter the next phase of my new career as a consultant. Perhaps that's all consultants are supposed to do, operate within a jargon and write reports devoid of substance. Its all make-believe.' I surmised.

Consultancy cannot just be muddles and jargon, building pieces are obviously necessary, but the peasant must be helped, hands-on, not bottom-up or top-down. A peasant wants sustenance, he wants advice, agricultural inputs and markets where he can get a fair price, not endless surveys, analysis and head counting. He is capable, often hardworking and diligent. A consultancy should do more than build institutions or refurbish rotting foundations. With these thoughts and mixed feelings I gave in my notice once my year was almost up and returned to England where Julia had gone to have our second child, Rachel.

Except for Jack probably everybody, including the priests and nuns I berated at every possible opportunity, breathed a sigh of relief at my departure.

Rebecca still difficult, returned with me, back to Chynance and Cornwall, away from hybrids and poverty and systems that did not work and a dictatorship who wanted a road and an Aussie Labour government who thought it a mistake. And hybrids which I never planted, what a failure.

*****

It wasn't long before GTZ the German development arm of the Ministry of Foreign Affairs contacted me concerning a project in Tanzania. Their enthusiasm over the telephone was inviting; 'With the World Bank we are going to rehabilitate the coconut industry in Tanzania. It is very long term, seven to ten years, are you interested in joining our team? Would you come for an interview? You have the right experience; please send us your CV.'

'I haven't got a CV, nor a typewriter, contact Jim Broom of Lever's Solomons, that should be good enough for you,' I responded.

They appeared enthusiastic. 'Come to Eschbon,' they said, 'we will write your CV here.'

So I went to Eschbon and was interviewed by an extremely pleasant crowd of civil servants, headed by Dr. Neddenriep who maintained a supervisory role over the project.

'We are going to plant coconut seed gardens in Tanzania for the purpose of producing hybrid coconuts for farmer use. They will pay for the seednuts. It is not a give away.'

'Why hybrids?' I query.

'Because they produce at least double that of local varieties.'

'How do you know?' I ask.

'Because the French have done extensive work on hybridisation techniques in the Ivory Coast and we can use their expertise.'

'There are no large scale commercial plantings of hybrids in the Ivory Coast, they are just demonstration plots. The success of hybrids on Lever's plantations in the Solomon Islands and from plantings in the Philippines has yet to be ascertained, yields are disappointing so far,' I tell him.

Silence.

Then followed a typical Germanic response. 'We are confident we will succeed.'

'They will be a valuable asset to the small farmers and large plantations of the country,' I was told firmly.

'No nonsense here,' I thought.

I am interviewed by an agreeable threesome who asked if I had any reservations concerning working with Germans.

'Absolutely none at all I replied; my uncle bombed you, my father fought you, my father in law sunk you in his little submarine. However, you appear, surprisingly, to be very pleasant people, as I am sure you all are.'

A wry smile, a fidget of slight embarrassment; I must be careful, after all I am looking for a job.

I did not expect to be offered the position of agronomist, but was. Julia was delighted for in quick succession she was pregnant again, this time with a boy, Frank, and realised that looking after three children in England, with limited help, was not exactly appealing.

I was still planting vines and had now employed a full-time ex-horticultural worker to help and also tend our commercial flower gardens.

I did not know Africa at all, although I had visited Kenya in 1972 and had entered Tanzania briefly and my father had served there before. I could never understand why the whites did not like the blacks very much and likewise the blacks did not care for the whites either, while neither particularly liked the Indians. Whereas in Malaysia, where I was living at the time, we all got on genuinely very well together or at least we tolerated each others' foibles without reflection to either race, colour or creed.

Tanzania here we come, I digressed, and signed my new contact. Julia was pleased, 'There must be music', she said.

16

A New Beginning

Life however was not easy during this period of the 1980s. Tanzania was experiencing hard times. The commercial world had imploded and there was little to buy in the shops except for an abundance of shoe polish, a gin replica called Konyagi and, if one was lucky, delicious hot mango chutney. Should your life depend on obtaining a lavatory seat or basin or even a car windscreen, then a visit to Kariakoo market in Dar es Salaam would be advised. There all the essentials for a household were available, no questions asked and, if the exact model was not in stock then it would be promptly procured, with brand name attached and, if you were very lucky, 'Property of Her Majesty's Government', could be seen stamped, emblazoned, to confirm it being genuine. Sometimes, instead, His Majesty rather than Her Majesty would be visible indicating antiquity.

Julia taught music at both the Dar Conservatoire and at IST (the International School of Tanganyika) and sang in the choir. There were recitals, for there was talent, singers, pianists, violinists, woodwind and others.

The musicians came from a variety of countries and backgrounds; a soprano with a beautiful voice was East German, the best pianist in town, the American wife of a German diplomat. Singers from every country and the Little Theatre provided entertainment of the highest calibre. Actors were talented amateurs. Productions were varied, the highlight of the year was the Christmas pantomime; as good as any production anywhere. The result, West End shows, performed as though the Little Theatre was a London stage.

There was indeed music in Dar es Salaam, the Conservatoire of Music flourished presided over by a Mrs. Lucy Croles-Reece, and, the Dar es Salaam choral society was exceedingly well supported.

*****

Tanzania's villagers generally fared better than town dwellers for they grew their own food and survived on a healthy diet, unless the rains failed and starvation plagued the countryside.

In the towns, procuring food was difficult, whether for a common person or government leader. It was not unusual to go to a Government office to find half the staff away planting their crops.

The only persons who managed to stave off hunger were the diplomats whose tax-free imports arrived in containers to the benefit of anyone who could get their hands on the choicest delicacies packed within.

Fortunately the vegetable markets thrived and it was an amazing logistic accomplishment that they were always well stocked, even though there was hardly any diesel to provide the transporters who trucked in the goods.

It was this trading capability of the Tanzanian, in difficult times that made it so perverse that the government should wish to inhibit their ability to compete by introducing socialist principals of commerce. For the average Mr. Tanzanian was completely adept at organizing and performing at a competent level complex marketing activities without assistance or resources.

His world was survival, his culture revolved around minimalism, which bred resilience to hardship that others in the richer world could not possibly begin to comprehend. Although the economy faltered badly during this decade, the only answer and advice provided to a beleaguered government by the overseas aid donors was state

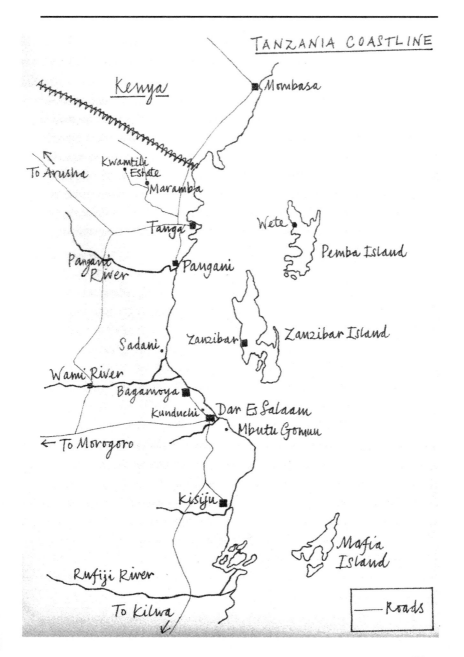

TANZANIA COASTLINE

Kenya   Mombasa

To Arusha   Kwamtili Estate
              Maramba

Tanga

Pangani River   Pangani

Wete   Pemba Island

Sadani   Zanzibar   Zanzibar Island

Wami River
Bagamoya   Dar Es Salaam
Kunduchi   Mbutu Gomun

← To Morogoro

Kisiju

Mafia Island

Rufiji River

To Kilwa

Roads

ownership and control of all industries. Everything the previous British administration had encouraged concerning development and commerce was swept away.

Tanzanians longed for economic stability, but the thrust of those agencies advising the government on economic affairs, for example the Scandinavians, particularly the Swedes, the Germans, East and West, who regarded Tanzania as their own fiefdom, the Russians, the Dutch, every country which had a mission, promoted their own social message with which they belaboured poor Mr. Nyerere and his government. Mr. Mao Tse Tung, China's communist leader, had become President Nyerere's best friend and most ardent supporter.

New systems of governance were explored and introduced; new thoughts, new ideas. Sweden's highly sophisticated welfare system, which provided unlimited help to the meek and lowly, was regarded as the definitive model to pursue and which would ensure the non-exploitation of all people. Many of the younger generation of civil servants had attended universities in Bulgaria, East Germany and Russia; some went to China and Romania, and to other seats of learning in eastern block countries. All returned indoctrinated with the teaching they had experienced. Tanzania was fast becoming an experimental classroom on socialistic governance.

It was a plethora of different approaches, of different ideologies of what was necessary and what was not. But no clear idea emerged as to how to manage the Tanzanian economy.

For President Nyerere's government it was a nightmare, as the economy became gradually ruined with the plantations and urban industries nationalised, only to be managed by ill-suited parastatals. Eventually there was nothing to sell and therefore nothing to buy. Socialism had failed the Tanzanians as it had done in other parts of Africa.

However, significantly, many of those who had become committed to their socialist experiences when studying abroad, even when a more capitalistic approach emerged, once President Nyerere had retired, still clung to the intransigent ideology of their eastern block education. At the same time they never appeared adverse to enjoying the fruits that often came their way through the infusion of aid money and a more open economy. For their political beliefs were seldom in conflict with the glittering baubles on offer from the western donors' munificence, nor the pursuit of new riches, as the economy began to revive and money became more readily available, particularly at the top end of society.

*****

Thus, in the late 1970s and early 1980s with the country bankrupt and in despair, the scene was set for the arrival of European and Asian aid agencies to prop up the Tanzanian government. Which helped, a little, but did not liberalize the economy and this resulted in a black market of currency exchange rates. In essence the unofficial rate of exchange became the rate by which all transactions were carried out.

Such was the situation in 1981, which heralded my entry into the perennial problem of how to solve Tanzania's economic ills.

It was all quite simple; grow coconuts, preferably hybrids. More coconuts meant more oil. There was a huge deficit, along with soap, toilet paper, rice, flour, butter, whisky, everything. Coconuts could sustain a household, it was the tree of life, every part of the palm yielded a product of some sort or other; oil from the albumen, timber for building a house or making furniture and the palm frond as roofing material. That was the message we proclaimed.

GTZ embarked on its project with fervour and diligence, as only the Germans can. Without doubt the National Coconut Development Programme (NCDP) was possibly the most publicised and talked about project during the 1980s. It had to succeed. But would it?

17

Under Surveillance

It was calculated that for a family to survive in Tanzania 70% of one's time needed to be devoted to searching for food, electricity, water and diesel and the other 30% performing the duties for which the company or agency were paying you.

We eventually rented a pseudo-Arab-looking house in Chato Street, Regents Estate, two miles from the city centre, belonging to whom, we knew not. A very personable housing agent found it for us and we moved in as quickly as possible.

It was not ideal, but there was occasional water and, provided you were on good terms with TANESCO (Electricity Suppliers) in your area, there was some power for the majority of hours in a day.

We loved the life, the children thoroughly enjoyed being in the tropics and while on safari (journey) for the project I was able to buy most commodities e.g. rice, sugar, flour and oil. My vehicle came back fully laden with provisions for ourselves and also for the staff who made sure my excellent, now deceased driver, Simon Mbollo, would return with plentiful supplies of maize, rice, bananas and cassava for distribution within our offices.

Our lives in Chato Street were consumed by the welfare of the children. Worms, dysentery and malaria were commonplace, Doctors were few and far between and there were no medicines. Julia became very adept at coping, there was no alternative. Supplies of food, soap, medicines and gin were air-freighted to us from Penzance. Sweets in the packages were meant to ease the children's distaste for chloroquin, an anti-malaria drug.

In the newspapers there was little good news to cheer about. Shortages hardly made the headlines, they were no longer newsworthy. However one disturbing piece of news concerned the thwarting of a coup attempt. Many were supposedly involved.

It was one afternoon, having returned from our offices in the TDFL building opposite the Royal Palm Hotel in downtown Dar that I received a telephone call from the Bank of Tanzania. As I received a number of calls concerning procurement of hybrid seednuts I was not surprised that somebody had telephoned asking for me and requesting that I go to the Bank. After all, every dignitary around Dar es Salaam now had imported hybrids growing in their gardens.

At the Bank I was asked to go to the basement, where to my surprise, I was questioned about the amount of rent I paid and to whom.

As they seemed to know the answers to most of the questions, my replies were merely confirmatory grunts. Except I refused to divulge who I paid the rent to, because in all honesty I did not know and I also gave a fictitious bank account number because I knew my bank would never agree to divulge such a (sacrosanct) piece of information.

It was only later during the interview that I was told the reason for my questioning; finance for the coup, who was responsible.

Although they knew my business was coconuts, specifically hybrids, as I reminded them, hopefully whetting their desire to put in a request for some themselves, there was no reason as far as they were concerned why I shouldn't have been involved. I tried to squash these disagreeable fantasies, replying that such a suggestion was highly unlikely being a married man with three children in an unfamiliar country working for GTZ and the World Bank. The latter paying my salary.

'So what?' they replied. 'You have a past.'

They were not at all unpleasant and after reiterating that I should not skip the country and that they were going to contact Interpol, I was allowed to leave. 'And your passport, where is that?' They called after me as I left the room.

'At GTZ's HQ,' I replied. 'Quite safe,' I reassured them and quickly emerged into the sunlight.

'Where have you been?' asked Julia. 'We have visitors.'

Four soldiers leant against the kitchen windows.

'Oh dear,' I thought, 'this is perhaps more serious than I first realised.'

The project leader, Dr. Speidel, was an extremely amiable gentleman with a good sense of humour. He had heard that some foreigners had been pulled in for questioning, although I was the first from NCDP. He would tell the German Embassy and I should tell the British High Commission. 'This is outrageous, unacceptable!' he blustered.

'Let's see what happens next,' I said to him. 'I will make sure Julia is ready to leave if I am compelled to stay. She and the children have their return tickets ready.'

I went for another interview. A repeat of the first, after which I heard no more.

Then, one day into my office, who should saunter in but my two interrogators. They eyed up my secretary and sat down.

'Thank you very much for the armed guards, they have kept the thieves and rogues away.' I greeted them politely.

'You have been cleared,' they said.

'Oh good, thank you for telling me, have you caught the culprits?' I asked. They ignored the question.

'These hybrids,' one asked, 'are they as productive as we are told?'
'Absolutely,' I replied, 'in four years you will get your first crop.'

'How do we get some?' they asked.

'Write your name down and address and you will be sent a sample, with a package of information.'

They got up to leave.

'If I were you,' one said, 'leave that house before you really do get into trouble, the owner and agent are in prison.'

18

The Greeks of Kunduchi

I searched high and low for another house until one day driving along the old Bagamoyo road north of Dar, I espied, perched on a hill, a cluster of old brick farmhouses. 'A plantation,' I thought, 'it must be sisal.' But as I approached there was little sisal to be seen, the estate seemed to be very run down.

I found a track, which circumnavigated a quarry and drove up it, passing by a chapel, then a large empty house and, further on to a more lived-in bungalow overshadowed by an enormous bougainvillea climbing up a baobab tree, under which lay panting dogs, snoozing workers, dozing cats and in the background squealing pigs; the bleating of penned goats and a large flock of sheep completed the menagerie. But no, not quite, for amidst this babble of inactivity stood two Greek statues, Dimitri Mantheakis and his son Dimi, quietly surveying the scene. They turned as I intruded upon their quiet reverie.

I stopped my vehicle and got out, no movement stirred the tranquillity. 'Good afternoon,' I said.

An arm was raised in a brief salute. I paused, should I disturb them, I considered.

'I was just passing by and wondered if you had a house to rent.' I asked hesitantly.

Dimitri raised his eyes and looked me up and down. He nodded his head as though deep in thought.

'You want a house?' he asked. 'Come,' he said, 'come,' and without further discourse led me back down the drive to the house I had just passed.

'Here,' he said, pointing. It was large and spacious with a huge encircling veranda.

'Come,' Dimitri beckoned me, 'come.'

He opened the veranda door and we walked around to the front where I was greeted with a magnificent view, the sea in the far distance.

It was unspoilt and the house appeared warm and welcoming. I would have to consult with Julia, but she would love the house, I was certain.

'Is there water?' I asked Dimitri.

'Oh yes, yes,' he confirmed quietly. 'Dimi will see to it.'

'Oh, oh perhaps it doesn't have water?' I questioned.

'Oh yes, yes there is water,' Dimi nodded agreeing but not convincingly. 'We will get you water,' he said.

'Is there electricity?'

'Oh yes, yes,' said Dimitri, 'there is plenty of electricity.'

As we were now in the house, we went into the kitchen and he turned on the main switch with a flourish.

'You see!' he exclaimed triumphantly.

There was no electricity.

'Dimi will get you electricity,' said Dimitri.

'When do you want to move in?' he asked.

'As soon as possible,' I replied, 'next week, if you agree.'

His slight nod, I took as indicating an affirmative reply.

'Come,' he said, 'come,' and off we ambled back towards their house. 'Now we will listen to the BBC and have a coffee.'

This was my introduction to the Mantheakis family and our home for six years and a friendship for the next twenty-five years, which still continues.

Chased by a hippo while crossing the Rufiji river

*****

The house belonged to Stella Kasamias, Dimitri's wife, who was now residing in Greece along with Louanna, the only daughter in this family of five sons. It was spacious and the veranda provided a running track and football pitch for the children. Outside, mango trees, citrus and cashew flourished and below on the hill slopes sheep and goats grazed amongst the rocky coral outcrops and a few defiant sisal plants. The plantation had once been 5,000 acres but much had now been nationalised and the family was only allowed to retain 100 acres for subsistence farming.

As our NCDP office had now moved to a new complex at Mikocheni just twenty minutes away and as Rebecca was attending the International School, half an hour's travelling time, our lives had taken a most agreeable turn for the better. We had become very much part of the Mantheakis' establishment. Probably the best known of the last of the remaining settler families in the country.

*****

Although life remained complicated in terms of procuring goods, my frequent safaris (journeys) did mean that I was able to take advantage of what was on offer by the roadside or in the village market place.

Very often Julia and the children accompanied me, loving the wildness of the landscape and the animals wandering the game reserves, free and content. The space and emptiness thrilled us all.

Owing to the difficulties of procuring fuel, travel was very much curtailed and there were few habitable lodges or camps. When I went on safari I would stay on farms or with friends, in the south of the country the Benedictine Brothers, who farmed their land productively and taught vocational skills to the local people, were always welcoming.

On one particular occasion I took Julia and the children with me to stay at Kilwa where there was a monastery. As we had to cross the Rufiji River, the Land Rover was ferried over on a small raft, vehicles only, while we were to cross by canoe powered by a dilapidated and ancient outboard engine fixed to the stern.

Needless to say the engine would not start and we drifted downstream, much to the annoyance of hippos whose peace we were disturbing. Suddenly one irate bull decided to chase us away and with considerable speed and nimbleness he submerged and stumped towards us blowing a trail of bubbles. This spurred the boat driver to try even harder and with a sudden jerk of the starting rope the engine sprang to life. Not too soon for the hippo erupted in a fit of turbulence and spray, much to the delight of Rebecca and Frank, but to nobody else.

*****

Although there was so much to enjoy in Tanzania, health problems for so young a family were cause for concern. Our children were still too young to have developed a combative immune system to Tanzania's parasitical and bacterial population, which would have lessened the debilitating effects of the usual tropical sicknesses, whether dysentery, diarrhoea or typhoid and of course the scourge of Africa, malaria. To combat these diseases Julia had to manage with limited medicines and usually without any medical help, for competent doctors were in short supply.

Once when returning from Tanga I found Rachel lying ill with amoebic dysentery. She had lost 12 lbs, a serious weight loss for a three year old. Julia was feeding her from dehydration packs, staying awake, hour after hour. I took over so that Julia could sleep.

Then one morning Rachel suddenly felt like eating. Her transformation from a stricken undernourished waif to a pink-cheeked, although wan, little girl, indicated that gradually the medicines and drips were beginning to work.

*****

Although thieving was usually accomplished with a minimum of violence, we felt secure up on the hill living amongst the Mantheakis family. We also had purchased a black Great Dane, a huge dog. Although slobbery and soft he was large enough to terrify anybody visiting the farm.

We all had guns and everybody in the district knew we had, and so did the police, who regarded the family with both respect and some misgivings. 'What would they do next?' they asked themselves, when the boys deposited a handful of thieves caught in the act of driving off half a dozen of Dimitri's sheep flock to sell in the village.

Retribution was heaped upon the robbers. 'We are doing your job,' claimed the boys. 'Here are a bunch of robbers, prosecute them. They are a danger to society.'

89

'They look in bad physical shape,' retorted the police, 'more mouths to feed, more paperwork, repair work to their injuries ...'

'They tried to get away,' cried the boys.

'... and hostile lawyers too. What next?' sighed the police inspector. 'It would have been better to shoot them,' he lamented, 'we don't have the facilities to lock them up.'

Over-zealousness by the public always caused problems.

'We don't have a budget to look after criminals,' cried the harassed policemen.

'Then what are you doing in the police force? Build a bigger jail!' shouted the boys, as they drove off back to the farm.

*****

One evening at our house, the boys Dimi, Michel and Minas, having returned from a security patrol around the farm, had come to our house for refreshments.

Guns were unloaded and we sat chatting, when Julia coming to join us, said, 'Either I have drunk too much gin or I am seeing things, for a bed sheet and pillow have just disappeared through the security screen bars.'

I jumped up and ran to the bedroom and sure enough slipping from the bed, across the veranda, through the mosquito netting surrounding the veranda, a fast disappearing sheet was being pulled by a fishing line with hook attached.

'Thieves!' I shouted, the boys jumped up and grabbed their guns. Michel went to the back door, Dimi to the front followed by Rebecca aged 6. I picked up my gun and with a yell we rushed down the hill after the thieves, presuming he or they had gone in that direction.

There were Greek shouts of battle tactics, followed by silence. I arrived by the road at the bottom of the hill to find Michel stopping bicyclists, pedestrians and lorries. There was not a thief in sight.

'Where is Rebecca?' I asked.

90

Cedar relaxing at Kunduchi

'I don't know,' came back the reply.

Oh God, I had lost Rebecca, although she knew the surrounding country as well as anybody, certainly better than me. I ran back to the house.

'Where's Rebecca?' asked Julia.

'I don't know,' I replied.

'Well we had better find her!' and out she bustled.

At that moment in stamped Rebecca.

'He is gone,' she said.

'Who?' I asked.

'The thief,' she said. 'in the opposite direction. He went backwards as everybody went frontward down the hill.'

I unloaded my gun.

'Where is Cedar?' (our Great Dane) I asked Rebecca.

'Oh he's fine,' she said.

'I hope he was of assistance?' I asked her.

'Well not exactly, he is fast asleep.'

I went round to the far side of the veranda, where Cedar with legs upright against the wall was snoring undisturbed, twitching in anticipation as he dreamed of protecting us from marauding robbers.

Julia was last to return, looking anxious.

'Oh thank heavens you have found her,' gasped Julia, panting for breath. 'She was with me all the time,' said Dimi, 'quite safe. You seem to be in a bit of a fluster.'

'Oh, no more than usual,' replied Julia.

That evening we lost two bed sheets and a pillow. The only other item that was ever stolen while living at the farm was an electric iron, without a flex.

The most bizarre attempted break-in occurred when Julia, entering the sitting room on her way to the study, found kneeling down beside the book shelves where her portable record player lived, a thief trying to operate it.

He looked up, startled by her entrance and, forgetting himself, cried out in frustration, 'It does not work!' before fleeing as Julia, shouting, 'Thief! Thief!' rushed to get her gun.

The thief departed in haste, as Julia, followed by the children, including Frank, who was by then three years old, chased him off the veranda and into the scrub and rocks below the garden.

The thief was not caught, but he never returned.

19

A Huge Success - First Stage

Up and down the coastal belt of Tanzania we travelled spreading the gospel according to hybrid coconuts.

The villagers were interested, as were the farmers and even some of the plantation owners. We managed to purchase a wide range of different varieties of hybrids from the Ivory Coast, which were air freighted to Tanzania at enormous expense. Some were distributed to the local authorities to raise in their own nurseries for farmer distribution and also to large-scale growers, state-owned and private companies.

We had many satisfied customers during this period and we began to feel that the hybrid would come out trumps and the yields we estimated would be achievable. The French inspired us to be confident. They knew, they said.

Two seed gardens were established, one on Zanzibar and the other on Mafia Island. It would still take time before the mother palms could be pollinated. Meanwhile imports from the Ivory Coast continued to satisfy the growing demand.

The Mantheakis family planted a grove on their farm, for Dimi was eager to make their land more productive. Smaller farmers included Dr. Kiwia, a chemist at the Wazo Hill Cement factory, the Benedictine Brothers and a whole range of public servants, including the former Director General of Police, Aziz Othman.

One old farmer planted his hybrids by a swamp close to Kisiju, four hours journey from Dar. One morning he arrived at the office deeply worried. 'My coconuts have been destroyed, come quick, now!' he said.

After filling up the vehicle with diesel we departed Dar and headed south. Rotten roads, huge pot holes, debris littered the surface and hindered our progress. At last we arrived, it was early evening.

'There!' he shouted. 'Look!'

Indeed the seedlings had been trampled down by heavy feet. I looked around searching for the cause. A black lump rose from the nearby river estuary, and then another.

'Hippos!' I exclaimed. 'The hippos are the villains.' He looked.

'Yes, you are right ... what now?' he sighed.

'What else do you do?' I asked him.

'I gather beche-de-mer, the sea slug, and sell it to the Chinese.'

'Well continue with that, I am afraid the hippos will return if you plant again.' He left us, despondent, sea slugs would certainly be a better option than coconuts I thought.

*****

The project was managed smoothly and, periodically, World Bank field officers arrived to inspect and report back on what was being achieved. Except for Julian Blackwood, who was diligent and knowledgeable, the others, a variety of continentals of poor pedigree, were more interested in acquiring antiques and carvings from Zanzibar than involving themselves fully in the project. And none knew anything about coconuts.

However it did not matter for under the competent management of Dr. Speidel, initially, and then Dr. Hubert the project went from strength to strength, with us consultants integrating well with our Tanzanian counterparts.

*****

One person who stood out above everybody else was my driver and personal assistant, Simon Mbollo, who was attached to me for the duration of my involvement in the project. He was quite excellent, not only as a driver and when promoted to the position of transport officer, but as a person who was totally reliable and trustworthy. I have never ever worked again with such an efficient and competent colleague.

I travelled far and wide, setting up demonstration blocks, promoting the majesty of the hybrid, soil sampling and examining areas worthy of development, inspecting existing groves of coconuts, advising farmers.

Simon always accompanied me. Should the vehicle breakdown, he was always able to repair it or, if he was unable to, knew somebody who could, even if we happened to be immobile in the thickest forest of the Rufiji River basin. He was incredibly resourceful and seemed to know everybody, or, was related to somebody who knew somebody who would assist. His spoken English was excellent and it was generally accepted that he may have been a ten cell member (an informer), the socialist way of keeping tabs on one's neighbours. But like many others he had become disgruntled with socialism as life got harder day by day.

Once I asked him to meet me at the Kigoma rest house at a specific date and time. Kigoma is located on the banks of Lake Tanganyika, at least three full days drive from Dar. He was there when I arrived, unhurried, always courteous. Sadly he died at Christmas 2004 of a heart attack.

20

Diversions

I was asked on occasions by other foreign and government agencies to provide a short-term agronomic input for them. There appeared to be a dearth of agronomists, (a title that I had now acquired, to be used henceforth as I periodically ennobled and embellished my CV).

Dr Speidel had no objection me going for a few weeks on short term assignments. It was good for the project that NCDP was called upon to provide assistance to other aid agencies, and of course it helped impress the Ministry of Agriculture that our consultants were in demand.

The family was now well ensconced in Tanzania so leaving them for a few weeks was not a problem.

*****

GTZ sent me to Ethiopia, where their officers were helping establish a commercial flower and vegetable enterprise. However this was not the purpose of my visit.

Bob Geldof, the singer, at the time was highlighting the terrible famine afflicting Eritrea, once an agriculturally productive sliver of land previously colonised by the Italians, but now cursed by a never ending conflict with Ethiopia which was hampering the aid effort and causing huge losses of life.

He conducted, for a while, a solo effort in attracting the rich nations to this conflict and the famine. A pop singer and a cause, probably he was the first to realise how celebrity status could be used effectively in propelling a calamity into the houses of TV's gawking masses residing in the rich nations of the world.

The end result was massive airlifts of food, clothing, seed and other essentials. In the U.K. the aged knitted balaclavas and jerseys, people gave money generously to his cause and the media paid attention to the plight of the refugees who streamed over the borders into Ethiopia to avoid starvation and the guns.

What to do with the refugees was of immense importance to the government of Ethiopia. Where to put them? Locations were surveyed, they had to be suitable for development, crop growing, raising livestock and of course for habitation. GTZ Ethiopia was asked to go to the Illubabor Province to ascertain whether this sun scorched, dry, hot province, stretching from the foot of the mountainous Kefa Province, bisected by the River Gila, through to the remote southern region of Sudan, could support a refugee population.

I joined the GTZ team in Addis Ababa and with ministry officials we set off for the Illubabor Province. It was a pleasant, interesting drive. The weather cool and the scenery mountainous with forested slopes and coffee cultivated on the foothills and in the valleys. We passed soviet military bases and airfields where some of Mr. Geldof's generous aid packages were being siphoned off to feed both the Ethiopian army and Russian military personnel. Lorries crammed with containers loaded at Addis Ababa airport hurried past us in the opposite direction to the waiting, starving Eritreans.

We moved into Kefa Province, the home of coffee growing. Although it was the dry season, the elevation of the region 2000 m - 3000 m ensured a cool pleasant climate. Shrouding light mists greeted us in the early morning and a jersey was necessary attire as we sat around awaiting a breakfast of hard, dark bread and delicious coffee, brewed painstakingly to be sipped slowly, while savouring the distinctive aroma of fresh beans.

*****

From Kefa we descended into Illubabor and stayed at Gambela, which was mainly inhabited by Russian engineers engaged in damming up the numerous river tributaries feeding the Nile. The principal aim of this programme appeared to be directed at antagonising the Egyptians by reducing the flow of the Nile. Egypt was once a good friend of Russia's in its non-aligned heyday, but was currently out of favour, a relationship which the Americans subsequently had embraced. Because Egypt now received the largest handout of American aid, Ethiopia retaliated by courting the Russians. It was similar to musical chairs, when the music stopped everybody changed chairs.

Nothing could possibly grow down here, we toured the province and physically boiled. Plant life was scant and the soils, mostly black cotton, were cracked by the searing heat. Acacia trees tried their best to stay alive, even the hardy gum arabic bushes looked decidedly sad as they fought for moisture. While cashew nut trees once planted close by now extinct villages soon became mummified, spindly corpses as the sun's rays hammered, splintered and cracked the trees' bark, sucking out every ounce of resin in the process.

'What do you think?' asked a ministry official.

'Impossible,' I replied, 'you can see for yourself, nothing can live here. Maybe during the rains, whenever, if ever, some cereals could be grown, but look at the landscape, even the thorn trees are only just surviving.'

They were not particularly pleased with my assessment. I had not finished. 'Surely you are not seriously considering bringing Eritreans here, who live in an equable, moderately temperate climate, influenced by the breezes from the Red Sea and the mountains within. They will die.' I said.

'They will die if they don't,' came back a terse rejoinder.

So there it was, within this land, nobody really cared what

happened, except of course Bob Geldof and the grannies in England. I returned to Dar es Salaam to write the required report, how could I influence the Ethiopian players, I wondered. In the end, fortunately, the Ethiopian government did not move the Eritreans to the Illubabor Province, but sadly Bob Geldof's aid did not reach them either in the quantities needed.

*****

In Tanzania I surveyed, for the Swedish Aid Agency, the Luichi Valley, close to Kigoma. Jan Lansler, a pipe-smoking economist, accompanied me, and made the pertinent observation when I queried him about how munificent the Swedes were towards Tanzania, that if one went to Church one never queried to which cause the money was allocated. Tanzania was the same and as far as the Swedish government was concerned, aid was charity to be used by the government as they wished.

We got on well and teamed up for a tobacco feasibility study later in the year, 1985.

For my last input in this sequence of assignments I was sent to Mafia Island, which I visited frequently for the coconut project and where I had struck up a firm friendship with the Manager, Adam Hill.

He tried his very best to manage a difficult situation where the owner, Henry Stanley, was in continual conflict with the surrounding villages owing to theft, and, also with me, because I was a member of the NCDP team and Henry did not like our hybrids, and being a Tanzanian citizen he was not at all enamoured with the direction the government was taking.

The Dutch, who had provided funds for the estate, wanted to obtain an impartial report. It was not difficult. The coconuts, non-hybrids, were yielding well and the herd of jersey cattle was producing abundant milk, processed into cream and cheese.

However funds were in short supply and once Adam's contract

ended the estate's survival became tenuous and eventually a mere shell of its former productive self. But that was the way things came to pass in Tanzania.

21

Mixed Fortunes

The project went from strength to strength, while Tanzania tottered from one economic crisis to another. There was a feeling of desperation, for the country had so much to offer. It was peaceful, socially content, without bias to any religion; tribal contentiousness did not exist and, like most agrarian people worldwide, blessed with old-fashioned courtesy. This contrasted positively to what was happening in neighbouring countries, where animosity between tribes and beliefs had led to fractured and discontented societies, resulting in terrible blood letting, a consequence of the rifts.

'If only the economy would improve, then life would be uplifted,' everybody cried. 'We cannot go on like this,' was a common theme. But we did, life continued, just.

Up on the hill at Kunduchi, the Mantheakis butchery, under Minas the eldest son's capable supervision, continued to sell the most delicious cuts of pork and lamb and often smoked meats and fish. Clientele from around Dar visited the farm to buy their meat.

For most, life was not easy. There were shortages of maize and beans and because the farmer was encouraged to sell only to the nationalised distributors or co-operatives, they seldom bothered to till and crop their land productively. They knew that if they should sell their crop to the government they would either be paid only a portion owed or they would have to wait far too long for payment, which they could ill afford to do.

It was the same for commodity crops. Cashew nuts had to be sold to the Cashew Nut Authority; likewise sisal, cotton, coffee and all major crops to their individual parastatals owners.

Tea and coconuts were exceptions; tea being a complicated crop to grow and process, and the hectarage too small with little smallholder participation. While coconut, being principally a smallholder crop, was hardly suited to nationalisation. A few coconuts harvested from a handful of trees planted in the back yard were not an issue. Although the half dozen existing coconut plantations became loosely attached to the National Agricultural Food Company (NAFCO) these plantations, needless to say, slid into insolvency when theft of nuts became endemic.

*****

The enthusiasm of coconut farmers, large and small scale, throughout the coastal belt and Zanzibar, for hybrids continued undiminished. On Zanzibar, which enjoyed a higher rainfall, ±1500 mm annually, hybrids became an immediate attraction, producing prolifically after four years. And on the mainland, owing to well-distributed seasonal rainfall during 1983-85, the young hybrid seedlings flourished. Farmers small and large applied fertilizer or manure and looked after them with tender loving care.

Towards the end of 1985 some of the initial plantings began to bear crop. The first nuts harvested were from trees planted at Wazo Hill Prison in 1980, where the abundance of free labour ensured pristine conditions. It was presided over by a bright, intelligent prisoner, A. Mwamasangula, whose sentence was about to draw to a close and being well-versed in the art of coconut husbandry, and much else, I took him on to assist me with my various activities. He was to became a very reliable assistant.

Nut harvests during the first years were excellent. Then they appeared to dip as though all the palm's energy had gone into the seedling's establishment and the initial years of bearing and, thereafter a decline in production became commonplace.

This was not helped by a very dry year in 1986. There were ominous signs that such conditions would be a major inhibiting factor to the palms' wellbeing and nut bearing potential. We waited anxiously to see how the hybrids fared up and down the country during these periods of chronic moisture stress.

22

Schooling Becomes a Priority

Our children spoke Swahili amongst themselves and mixed freely with the farmworkers' children and also our cook Regina's young family. Rebecca daily tended the sheep and goats after school and would remain outside in the dusk until nightfall before agreeing to come inside to bath and sleep.

'We cannot go on like this,' I said one evening to Julia, 'they must be educated.'

'They are being educated very well!' retorted Julia.

'But it is not enough, for example, Rebecca wants to spend the rest of her life shepherding the farm's livestock. There is a competitive world out there.'

'Not for her there isn't,' replied Julia.

'And, Frank, he thinks that there are hippos in the stream at the bottom of our garden in Cornwall. He is now four years old and spends most of his time romping around, being fed mango flies, killing lizards and insects. This has to stop.'

We prepared to leave Tanzania in 1988 to many cries of anguish.

'They have got to go to school and realise they cannot spend the rest of their lives running wild in this picturesque oasis of bliss,' I insisted.

'It is alright for you!' exploded Rebecca, 'You can return.'

She was right, GTZ had agreed that I could still provide a short-term input annually.

'And, what about Cedar? He will hate England.'

Cedar returned later, in 1989.

'Anyway,' I tried to console the children, 'Stella will be returning and she will want her house back. I think none of us would like to live anywhere else but here.'

For us all it was unthinkable to live somewhere else, Kunduchi and the farm and the Mantheakis family were home to us. So for the last time in that house we organised a musical evening and a party.

Dimitri roasted three sheep and we searched around Dar for beer, wine and spirits, which were becoming more freely available from expatriate duty free shops now springing up around town and in Zanzibar. There we could buy imported goods, provided we paid in dollars and did not mind that the proceeds were being used to support regimes of dubious character in the Middle East and European charities of intemperate persuasions.

The party was a success. All the musicians from the conservatoire came, the choral society set and friends and neighbours. Those who played and sang, including my niece Ellen who was visiting us, enjoyed performing, for the high ceilings heightened the exceptional acoustics, the resonance being almost spiritual in its effect. The music resounded throughout the house. It was a magical evening, highlighted by Stella's presence, as she had returned for a brief stay and this of course added a special poignancy, for we were handing back to her, her house, which we had come to love so much.

Sadly we returned to Cornwall for the children's schooling. Had we made a mistake? I don't think so, little white Africans cannot run wild forever.

*****

I did return when the project still prospered and then again in 1993 when after two further severe years of drought the project, agriculturally, had collapsed; the hybrids were unable to survive the dry years of 1991 and 1992. Even the EAT palms (East African Tall) suffered during this period.

All the hard work had come to nothing. The disappointment was palpable amongst the farmers and the government officers who had been so involved with the project.

Few hybrids, in this year, 2008, remain. The grove on the Mantheakis farm tries resolutely to survive; fronds drooping as if in disappointment, trunks slender and malnourished, one or two nuts only dangling from sparse inflorescences. A failure, palm-bearing longevity hardly 10 years instead of 100 years.

The project was an example of how a well-managed enterprise did not succeed. We had not understood the commercial exploitation of hybrids sufficiently, but then probably because hybridisation was such a new venture nobody else was entirely aware of their physiological shortcomings either. Certainly IRHO in the Ivory Coast never provided any indication that hybrids could fail. Drought conditions in Tanzania were the principal factor for their non-performance, but as Henry Stanley of Mafia Island once pronounced, better by natural selection than by using an artificial technique i.e. mating, probably, incompatible parents, dwarf with tall. The end result, many dissatisfied and disillusioned farmers and government officials.

23

Back to the East

I was fortunate that tropical tree crop agronomists were not in abundance, consultant agencies frequently phoned up and asked for my input, which could be six weeks to three months in duration.

Some were out of the ordinary.

'Would I advise on coconuts in Salalah (Oman), very pleasant climate?'

'That's next to Yemen isn't it? How's the fighting?'

'Oh yes, it is just over the border, stable, we think.'

Why would anybody want to grow palms in Salalah? I wondered.

'There is a project in Madagascar on vanilla. You know about vanilla don't you?'

'Of course,' I replied.

I hear nothing further about vanilla in Madagascar.

'Will pepper grow on the Isabel Islands of the Solomons?'

'Yes, I have just come from there.'

'Please go and report.'

I go and return.

And then...

'We have a problem in Baluchistan, one of the current crop of Tribal Chiefs wants to plant tropical tree crops in the mountains, could you please go there and persuade him not to.'

'I will try,' I replied.

I arrive in Karachi and journey on to Islamabad to meet the World Bank representative.

'Why don't you just tell the tribal chief not to plant oil palms or rubber, or, whatever, on the mountain tops, rather than call up somebody like me to come all the way from England?' I ask.

Not that I mind, I am very much looking forward to this mission.

'Because,' the World Bank representative answered, 'I happen to be a Pakistani; of the wrong tribe, wrong colour, wrong creed and probably, according to him, an Infidel, because I don't pray five times a day. That is why we have asked for somebody like you to advise him. Good luck!' he offered, as I left his office.

Next day I landed at Quetta where I was met by Roland Piers Groves who appeared to be trying to plant apples and pears in the most forbidding of landscapes. He was very welcoming and took me to the Tribal Chief's house which had been inhabited by the last British Chief Justice during colonial times.

On the lawn outside, surrounded by almond trees, a large marquee had been erected, in which the Tribal Chief now resided and held court. We entered, he spoke very good English.

'What is your name?' he asked, I told him.

'I knew a Babs Bryant at Cambridge, very good sportsman, soccer blue, are you related?'

I replied in the affirmative, which pleased him and he reminisced quietly about his life.

'Why are you here?' he asked.

Piers Groves entered the conversation;

'He has come to assist in the tropical tree crop programme and where they should be planted and advise your government officers accordingly.'

'I need no advice!' came back a brisk retort.

Meeting a tribal chief of Baluchistan

A pause followed.

'Well?' he turned to me, 'can I grow tropical tree crops here?'

Having been barely one day in Quetta I was hardly in a position to answer, but looking out at the barren, mountainous land beyond the haven of his tent and feeling the sharp cold bite of crisp air, planting tropical tree crops was, I felt, not a favourable option to pursue.

'No, not here, the plants would die of exposure, definitely inadvisable,' I said. He did not stir.

'Well where then?' he asked.

'Further down,' I latched onto my previous last minute research of the region just before departing from England. 'How about Jacobabad and the Sind?'

These territories were not under his jurisdiction, but he accepted my reply that the mountains were not the most suitable habitat for either oil palms or rubber.

Probably being the son of Babs Bryant had helped, for he turned to me as we left and said, his eyes glinting, 'Babs was a first class cricketer and soccer player but I always beat him at squash.'

*****

Son like father, everybody in Quetta beat me at squash, including Piers Groves and a previous World Champion who was at least seventy years old and had one leg. It appeared that Quetta was inhabited by a host of world champions, past and present, who had nothing else better to do than play the game morning, noon and night.

Quetta appeared very male-dominated. Few women were visible in town whether during the day or at night-time. While handsome, languid, pink-cheeked young boys were commonplace.

Early morning, should I be breakfasting at my favourite small corner eating shop, I watched, amused to see them scurrying away from previous night's assignments, their beauty enhanced with rouge and lipstick, on their feet high heeled shoes and slung over their shoulders well-oiled rifles. They appeared certainly more glamorous than their sisters, if you should ever be lucky to glimpse one.

My advisory role after that first morning was now in jeopardy, I had accomplished everything I had to in this particular phase of the consultancy and I had only been here a day or so. I had to embellish my terms of reference (TOR).

'Well, write up this part of your report now and we will then go and see what's happening in the rest of the country,' said Piers Groves.

It is difficult to write a regulation length report after one day's work which should have taken much longer but didn't. Spicing it up was necessary and with Piers Groves' help, including what he was doing, and how the Tribal Chief was trying to build up an integrated authority and that women in development (WID) was not even a consideration, thankfully, I finished the report, mentioning how difficult it had been to get the Tribal Chief's consent. 'I have achieved something,' I thought, 'I wish all consultancies were like this.'

I tried to telephone Julia, but couldn't.

'We will send her a message from head office,' Piers told me, 'it's the only way, there are no BT kiosks out there.'

Unfortunately, iridium satellite telephones, one of which I later procured, were still not part of the worldwide communication system.

Driving down the Bolan Pass

24

To Jacobobad

We visited many farmers in the district and then it was decided I should leave for Jacobobad. No systems, no institutional building, no flow charts to impress and sustain a tiny empire had so far interrupted my travels and rural visits. Instead eager farmers; 'What can we grow?' 'What trees should we plant on these sands?' '... gravels?' '... on these terraces?' '... in the valley bottoms?' 'How deep should the drains be dug?' 'At 10,000 ft will rubber grow?' 'What about coconuts here and betel nut there?' 'Markets, where are the markets?'

I enjoyed the buzz of farmers asking their incessant questions about agrarian survival and a little bit left over to buy a sheep or save for a dowry. The officials were also interested, for they owned land or belonged to a village which would also benefit from any agricultural progress.

At last I was using my experience and knowledge gained from twenty-five years in tropical agriculture. Utilising it for a purpose, to advise and assist these farmers, mostly poor, scraping a living on porous soils with little rainfall and extremes of temperature, and, wells, once 1 metre deep, now 30 metres. 'Water, water, it is getting drier every day,' came the cry.

We prepared to depart from Quetta, via the Bolan Pass, and head down to Jacobobad.

*****

Our small convoy descends stopping every four hours in order that the contingent of soldiers accompanying me can pray. Piers Groves has decided to stay behind in Quetta and will meet me later in Karachi.

As Baluchistan is full of warring tribesmen, it is decided, that for my own protection, soldiers should accompany me. My feeling is that stopping off to pray is a distinct disadvantage to my safety. The road is very exposed with mountains rising precipitously from the kerb and therefore offering excellent vantage points for a sniper wishing to exact revenge for the death of a brother or comrade.

The fact that I, son of Babs Bryant, sportsman, ex-friend and university associate to the current principal Tribal Chief of Baluchistan, who is also travelling with the convoy and has no desire to be shot at while awaiting his escorts prayers to be answered, probably is of little concern to the waiting tribesmen high up above me, watching.

We eventually reached Jacobobad, where a contiguous irrigation scheme had been a colonial venture of some magnitude. It had been an uneventful journey, highlighted by the splendour of the mountains either side of the pass and the incongruous sight of camels being transported on the back of trucks and pick-up wagons to Quetta for the summer grazing, where they would stay and then later return to the lower regions of the province for the winter season.

By late afternoon our small convoy halts outside an ancient rest house, nestling amongst woodland some distance from the town. It is of a past era; an unkempt garden surrounds the house, once upon a time an abode of substance and repose.

An old retainer bustles out to greet me. He takes my bag and ushers me in while the soldiers depart to the local barracks.

The rest house inside is beautifully airy and my bedroom huge and cool. Downstairs there is an elegant, although slightly dishevelled, drawing room, with an expected assembly of shorn heads adorning the walls. These were once attached to the torsos of the many varied species of the deer family which used to roam these parts, but now

At the rest house

sadly exterminated in the name of sport and farmer encroachment.

Underneath one of these unlucky heads sits the only other guest, Raman ul Haq, a forester on his way back to Karachi. I join him and sit down on a faded, worn out sofa. He greets me and we talk of our travels and work; his position as Chief Forester appears to encompass an area the size of Ireland.

The old retainer comes into the room to ask about dinner and at what time it should be served. He brings delicious tamarind juice with traces of cinnamon; Raman hesitates, then leans closer;

'Would you like a beer?' he asks. I nod the affirmative.

'Could you then ask the old man,' he requests, 'it is better that you ask, rather than me.'

'You will have one too, I hope,' I jocularly ask.

'Of course,' he says, 'many, if possible.'

I ask the hovering retainer if he could bring us beers. He bows slightly, and departs. It is not long before two very cold bottles appear. These are poured into long stemmed glasses, extracted from a heavy wooden cabinet, in which a whole range of glassware and china has been carefully placed.

Raman looks at the foam and then putting the glass to his lips takes a long draught. Ecstasy radiates across his face. I drink too, it is probably the most satisfying beer of my life.

Dinner is a delicious curry, served with aplomb as though the old retainer is continually in practice. However from the ancient visitors register guests are not frequent, except by one senior army officer whose name is prominent and, as Raman whispers, probably due to the abstemious nature of the country, he comes for the beer supplied by this admirable old servant.

*****

My stay in Pakistan was drawing to a close and I spent my last few days in the Sind. Wherever I travelled, each and every farmer wanted to show me some plant he was lavishing attention upon. Accompanied by an agricultural officer we drove for four hours to visit a farmer who was growing six cardamom plants in his backyard, shaded from the searing heat by palm fronds. He was very proud of his achievement. He wanted more and could I help? I would try, I said. And a farmer attempting to grow coconuts in a drained swamp.

'Would they live?' I was asked.

'Probably but dig deeper drains or they will die.'

The question of where they could get seed, or plants or cuttings always arose. Spices were much in demand, but none would grow without irrigation I would advise. Water, water, markets, a plea for help.

Fortunately by the time I was back in Karachi Piers Groves had arrived and we discussed how the farmers could get their hands on the many varied exotica they were interested in cultivating.

Seed merchants and horticultural nurseries were visited and with the help of a local agricultural officer we established a network and provided a range of addresses in the Far East, especially the Philippines, where planting material could be obtained with the necessary phytosanitary requirements supplied.

'We will have to try and organise a review mission,' insisted Piers Groves, 'to make sure that the horticultural merchants have managed to procure all these different species of plants at the cost agreed.'

I never went back to Pakistan, but I did meet Piers Groves again in Jakarta when I was involved with the transmigration project. He was still working as an agricultural consultant and asked if I would come to Cambodia to join him there. I received a TOR which seemed extraordinarily vague, and a plane ticket but nothing else. Piers Groves was surprised that I did not turn up at Phnom Pen as he had been told to expect me.

Going to Sunday market in the Russells. Solomon Islands 1978.

Rebecca learning to swim in the Russells, 1978.

Feast time at Yandina on Independence Day, 1978.

Julia's cowboys at Yandina on Independence Day.

Independence Day at Yandina on the Russells, 1978.

Malaitans dancing at the Independence Day celebrations, Yandina 1978.

N. Samar Province outside Cataman, 1981.

Village houses in N. Samar.

Stella's house at Kunduchi where we lived for six years. 1982 Tanzania.

The Greeks. Left to right: Dimi, Mikalli, Michael, Dimitry (father), Yani.
(absent, Minas, Platton and Louanna)

Regina and family plus Rebecca, Rachel and Frank at
Kunduchi. 1983. Tanzania.

On Safari in the Selous Game Reserve, waiting for Frank. 1984.

Land unsuitable for coconuts.

Enjoying the freedom of Kunduchi with Cedar our great dane.

East Kalimantan 1990. The little old lady past her best.

Muara Wahau jetty. Our children.

Dayaks celebrating Christmas 1990 at Muara Wahau village.
Rebecca in foreground.

Muara Wahau village.

Kuching. Governor's office in background, multi storeyed.

A river scene in Sarawak.

Kwamtili estate house. Tanzania.

Rachel at Kwamtili. Christmas 1998.

Kwamtili estate offices, factory (left) and hospital.

Ramathani. Kwamtili estate.

Kiwanja Mbutu. Tanzania 2000.

Dancing at Mbutu. Julia and me.

Christmas party at Stella's. Rachel, a friend, Rebecca and Frank.
Tanzania 2000.

25

Transmigration

A solution was needed to find an answer to the over population problem in some provinces of Indonesia, particularly Java. Cultivable land was limited while at the same time the population was spiralling ever upwards. Something had to be done.

It came to pass that after many years of deliberation, a grandiose plan was authorised by which the poorest farmers living in those regions severely overburdened with teeming masses of people would be relocated to areas where there was surplus land.

The plan became known as the Transmigration Scheme and during the late 1970s and 1980s was the principal vehicle through which the resettlement of the poor, urban and rural, and, landless peasants, was brought about. The project was funded by the World Bank.

It was a bold idea for it necessitated the clearing of extensive tracts of unused and unpopulated land, usually secondary jungle, in remote regions of the country, Sumatra and Kalimantan principally. Once cleared, migrants would then be moved into these deforested areas by boat and lorry to inhabit, cultivate and plant their crops.

Each settler family at a scheme was provided with a rough wooden house, sufficient land to grow their crops and for the first 6-8 months, a food package adequate to keep the family fit and well while they cultivated their land to ensure their future food supply.

In order to provide employment and a cash return, commodity crops, oil palms and rubber were planted and coconuts latterly. This was performed using estate plantation techniques rather than a programme of random smallholder plantings.

Much criticism was heaped upon the schemes, especially by NGO's, human rights activists, and even the Economist Magazine, all of whom were concerned that many of the settlers were being forcibly coerced to migrate. Also much of the land selected was not considered particularly suitable; often elevated with a shallow topsoil, or flat plains of heavy clays, glutinous when wet, requiring intensive drainage. Consequently dire predictions of famine and pestilence were heaped upon the transmigration schemes, frequently referred to as expensive · failures.

However, the schemes provided a dwelling place for the migrants and a new start to life. As most were Javanese, hardworking, diligent and competent, they soon had irrigated rice fields operating with hand dug irrigation channels interlinking over the fields and simple sluice gates built to control the flow of water. Their genius in creating paddy fields was to be admired and on some schemes rice, rather than the commodity crops, became the main source of income. The dire predictions of failure were unfounded.

*****

It was impressive and when I visited schemes in the late 1980s and then the same ones in 1996 and 1998 I was struck by the progress. New villages had been created, towns with mosques, shops, offices and cinemas had been built where only jungle existed before. These schemes were successful.

While many transmigration schemes flourished, a few unfortunately failed, leaving behind destitute collections of shacks, from where the male migrants had departed to find work elsewhere; their women folk left behind tilling their backyards to provide sustenance to the ever increasing numbers of children born annually and without respite.

The stoicism of the settlers was remarkable and, despite the continual meddling by government officers, endemic corruption and general mismanagement, they applied their skills as best they could and often to a high level of competence. Resulting, in many cases, that after ten plus years some of the farmers would sell their smallholdings, most of which now consisted of brick-built homes and well cropped fields and with the proceeds they elected to return to their villages of origin.

Although such commercial transactions were not in the original script, it showed how the schemes had become successful, due almost entirely to the resourcefulness of the settlers, supported by World Bank money.

I was involved on six transmigration schemes during the period 1987-1990, advising on both commodity crop and arable crop selection and husbandry. In 1990 I was asked to provide an agronomic input for two transmigration schemes located at Muara Wahau and Sangkurilang in East Kalimantan. The implementing activities were to be performed by PTP VI (Perseroan Terbatas Perkebunan VI), a state-owned plantation enterprise, although previously a pre-independence Dutch plantation company.

26

Muara Wahau and Sangkurilang

A Dutch firm had won the contract for my agronomic input and as I could speak Indonesian, which is similar to the Malay language, they were extremely eager for me to get started. They were a no nonsense outfit, aggressive and penny-pinching, but once you got to know them considerate and well-meaning.

I departed for Indonesia; Julia was to follow once the children had been settled into boarding school, that very British institute of learning.

I had been to E. Kalimantan before and knew the schemes to be isolated. In the case of Muara Wahau, reachable only by river transport, while the journey to Sangkurilang, located on the East Coast some distance from the town of Bontang, necessitated a sea trip by boat and then by vehicle along rough tracks which sliced through the equatorial forest of the Province.

*****

I arrived in Jakarta and, after meeting with my employers, sauntered down to the World Bank offices in Kuninggan, Central Jakarta.

The Mission Head was a pleasant Australian who tried his best, although bureaucratic interference by the involved authorities must have made his life very frustrating indeed.

'Why plant coconuts at Muara Wahau and Sangkurilang? The soils are too clayey and coconuts don't like deep impervious soils. Better oil palms or rubber,' I said. 'And, this is surely the first time coconuts have been used as a commodity crop for a transmigration scheme. Is that wise?'

'Coconuts were decided upon during the feasibility study stage carried out by a Philippine Consultancy Group. And, also the hybrid coconut breeding station at Palawan, an island of the Philippines archipelago has millions of hybrid seednuts to sell, thereby providing the project with a readily available source of cheap planting material,' he answered petulantly 'and a visiting Bank agronomist has agreed that the location was suitable for coconuts, and, as you haven't been there, your pre-meditated surmises could be inaccurate.'

'We will see,' I said, and flew off to Balikpapan in E. Kalimantan, where I took a speed boat from Samarinda, arriving after seven hours of travelling at Muara Wahau village. It was a long hot, uncomfortable journey, for the speedboat had no canopy and the sun shone brightly. The tedium of the journey was only relieved by eating enormous succulent prawns at a riverside longboat which lay anchored straddling the equator at the convergence of the rivers Belagan and the Telan. My plate of rice lay south of 0° latitude while the prawns lay enticingly on a plate north of the line.

I was met at the project site by the Team Leader responsible for surveying the scheme and the other consultants, who were eager to leave once PTP VI, the implementing agency, and myself had taken up residence.

'Why ever are we planting coconuts on these soils when rubber or oil palms would be better suited to the conditions?' I asked, after we had toured a representative portion of the scheme.

'Well,' came back the reply, 'the hybrids are cheap to purchase, there are existing oil mills in Samarinda and the advice comes from a Philippine Consultancy Company who know all about coconuts but nothing about rubber or oil palms.'

'And how are we going to transport the nuts to Samarinda?' I asked.

'By barge...' came back the grimaced reply.

'And, what if the scheme is a failure? Hybrids have to date not earned a good reputation,' I said.

'Well at least the settlers, hopefully, will have enough food and cooking oil,' he answered.

The team leader was aware of the problems and also was not impressed with the decision to plant coconuts.

*****

I spent a few more days looking over the scheme and then flew back to Jakarta. I went from the airport straight to the World Bank offices. The Head of Mission looked bleak as I entered his office.

'Told you so,' I said cheerfully, which did not help his mood. 'The soil is just not suitable for coconut establishment. Of course, if planted in the settler's backyard they will probably survive, but as the major component to smallholder financial stability, coconuts are definitely not recommended. We have had problems with hybrids in Tanzania, also hugely in the Philippines, and I am certain they are no longer being planted in the Solomons. It is a new crop, still unproven. Who from the Bank agreed that hybrids would be suited to conditions at Muara Wahau?' I asked.

There was a pause and then from behind me a quiet voice answered 'I did.' I turned and espied a youngish man from the Indian subcontinent standing close by, there were many now ensconced in the World Bank hierarchy. 'Why?' I asked.

'Well the area could grow fodder crops, such as lucerne and other species of Gramminae very well, so why not coconuts? Similar root systems, just a difference in size.'

I looked at him, stunned, and uttered a rude expletive.

'I also have a PhD in grasses,' he was disarmingly polite, 'but not coconuts,' he admitted, not at all disconcerted by my abruptness.

The Head of Mission was not happy with the way the conversation was heading.

'There is a contract signed for implementation, nothing can be changed now,' he said, 'let's hope they grow, you must understand the consultancy report was adopted in good faith by the government and us, so there is little else we can do about it. And, the settlers at this moment are on their way.'

'Understood,' I said, 'but surely we should look again at the contract regarding shipping the nuts down to Samarinda by barge. It is just not feasible; there is time to find a new solution.'

He nodded, 'This can be discussed later once PTP VI are well settled into the implementing phase.'

'Oh dear,' I thought, 'here we go again, wrong crop, wrong place; selected because the planting material can be easily sourced, but still unproven. Close by. Agreed upon by somebody who has a doctorate in grasses; the crop to be shipped to oil mills in Samarinda, the owners, many of whom enjoy political connections have therefore a vested interest in river transporting their raw material downstream; another mess which could have so easily been avoided.'

27

The Schemes

I rented a pleasant house in Samarinda belonging to the mayor and then went up to Muara Wahau to start my consultancy.

PTP VI was managed by a nice young Indonesian, P. Tarigan, who had no experience of coconuts but like many Indonesian plantation managers, was able to adapt his vision and organisation skills to huge projects, managing heavy equipment and massed labour with considerable ingenuity, competence and alacrity. It was impressive.

Once a development phase got going, Indonesian plantation companies performed at a speed and purposeful intent that no Malaysian company could ever match.

The newly arrived hybrid seednuts from Palawan were laid out in nurseries, while the secondary forest was felled and burnt and made ready for the seedlings. The smoke from the fires and, from other plantation projects, was soon picked up by satellite, resulting in cries of outrage from Singapore complaining of pollution.

The migrants, who were now settled in make shift villages, commenced planting their crops in the allocated land and their paddy fields soon took shape, tended with care by the settlers, especially the majority Javanese.

At Sangkurilang work was behind schedule, due principally to the racial mix of non-agrarian migrants who had been selected for the scheme and, although the few Javanese on site performed with their customary flair, others of different ethnic stock e.g. those from the

Flores Islands, the East Timorese and those migrating from the islands of Sumbawa, appeared disinterested and lacked intent, ability and energy. Particularly those families from E. Timor who were without the basic agricultural skills necessary to be good farmers. However, they enjoyed planting flowers and making their gardens pleasing to the eye and some were quite talented musicians. They went to church every Sunday and appeared very much under the influence of the Roman Catholic priests who administered, rigorously, to their spiritual and earthly needs. They survived on the food parcels issued and produce harvested from their little gardens. They seldom worked and their lives were spent sitting around aimlessly and gossiping, having adopted the languid customs of their former rulers, the Portuguese.

To reach Sangkurilang from Muara Wahau was not easy as the main logging road to the scheme was poorly maintained and during heavy rains slippery and hazardous.

I was provided with an old Toyota Land Cruiser, well-constructed although heavy, lacking the agility that a Land Rover possessed. My driver, Lasar, a Dayak from Muara Wahau, was young and inexperienced and we spent many wearisome hours trying to extract ourselves from roadside ditches and quagmires into which we slithered and skidded as Lasar, grappling with the steering wheel, appeared incapable of following coherently the contours of the track and keeping a middle course. Our regular misadventures multiplied should the logging roads be wet after rain.

Still the journey was pleasant, the climate early morning refreshingly cool as the forest trees blocked out the sunlight. Monitor lizards over two metres long enjoyed resting in the middle of the road, and pigs in large herds used the tracks as access for their foraging. We drank from the streams and rested on the rocks before setting off again to negotiate another rib-rattling piece of track.

High above, monkeys gibbered and scrambled as we motored deep into the forest and in the evening hornbills and fruit bats winged above

Borneo - Kalimantan, Sarawak and Sabah

Mountains   △ G. Murud   = Provinces

Towns : Bontang   Sibu
         Samarinda   Miri
         Balikpapan   Kota Kinabulu
         Kuching   Pontianak
         Bintulu

Villages : Sangkulirang   River Mahakam
           Muata Wahau

Pushing out our vehicle in the jungle

from one favoured canopy to another.

We usually reached Sangkurilang by afternoon teatime, hot and bothered. I was provided with a nice airy room above the main office. It was cool in the evenings and mornings, with mist from the jungle floating over the coconut plantings and shrouding the migrant villages before being dispersed by the hot rising sun

*****

At both schemes wild boar incursions were endemic. They arrived in herds, snorting and rampaging through the plantings, brown and hairy with sharp tusks protruding from the side of their jaws, scuffing up the planted seedlings and eating the coconut albumen inside the nut.

Poison, Temik, was mixed in baits and applied around the seedlings. This worked well but being dangerous to humans, the poison was banned and no other substitute was found to be effective.

The army, which had a post at Muara Wahau, were called into shoot the invading wild boars but, being mainly Muslims, the idea of pursuing pig was anathema to their beliefs, so we recruited Dayaks to hunt the animals, but not possessing guns they made little progress in reducing the daily incursions.

Eventually we erected fences separating the worst affected areas, then cleared by bulldozer all neighbouring bush and secondary forest, thereby reducing the natural habitat of the pig. In this way we managed to effect a better measure of control.

*****

A World Bank project inspection visit took place. The agronomist, a Malaysian Chinese, Teoh Peng Kong, was knowledgeable and experienced. I knew him reasonably well before; he had been a Visiting Agent for Guthrie's Plantations.

'Why ever are you planting coconuts here?' he asked me, when we were visiting the schemes.

'It will take too long to explain,' I answered, 'I suggest you read the feasibility study.'

'I have,' he replied sourly.

'Then you know the reasoning behind it.'

'I don't like hybrid coconuts,' he continued, 'they are not showing the results that were expected.'

'I know,' I said. '... And what are you going to do about it? And the transport question too? Sending nuts to Samarinda is not a good move. We should build mills here and ship the oil to Bontang, that is if there is any oil.'

'Let's discuss this in Jakarta,' he responded.

*****

A meeting was held in Jakarta to ascertain the next move concerning nut transportation. The Philippine Consultancy Group was present, armed with figures detailing how bringing down the nuts by barge would be more cost effective than building an oil mill.

'Have you seen the river after heavy rain?' I asked the group.

'Wait until the waters subside,' they suggested.

'Impossible,' I replied, 'as you are aware, this is the tropics, the scheme is surrounded by jungle, rainfall is 2000 mm annually. There is only one dry season. The river is swollen for nine months out of twelve and rapid during seven months, there are currents and rocks. We would lose nuts and barges and that would be unacceptable.'

There were arguments and suggestions and counter suggestions.

'We need another feasibility study to seek a solution out of this dilemma,' requested one participant.

'Who is going to pay?' asked Teoh.

'We have the facts and figures,' I declared, 'it does not require another feasibility study; the river rises, it is rapid, boats would run aground on the rocks. We would lose nuts, it is as simple as that, why on earth do we need another study?'

More fees was the answer. A feasibility study meant fees. The WB Head of Mission who chaired the meeting was well aware that another study was eagerly being sought after by those interested parties present.

'Can you do a feasibility study?' he asked me.

'I have just told you,' I said, 'what more is required?'

'I applaud brevity, but take every aspect into account and make sure it is unbiased,' he replied.

I snorted my annoyance at his comment.

'Of course, of course,' I said, 'I am a planter, the report will be fair.'

'This project has not started well ...' whispered Teoh alongside.

The meeting closed, Teoh and I left.

'I wish I was back on the estates,' he said, 'everybody was so much more upright and straightforward and efficient.'

My inscrutable Chinese colleague looked wistful as I took him to the airport to fly back to Washington.

28

Christmas 1990

Samarinda will not be in any guidebook as a place to visit. It is a town without style, bulldozed out of the jungle, built of concrete slabs, interwoven with a network of fetid drains, which overflow during heavy rain.

In the more upmarket districts look alike chocolate box structures coated with icing sugar and roofed with red painted tiles, as if copied from a fairy tale picture book, rise haphazardly around the edge of the town to provide housing for the merchant classes.

A busy dock loads and unloads cargo throughout the day and night, particularly timber products. Close by, Chinese traders haggle over prices, and, markets selling every kind of ware encourage, energetically, the shoppers to buy.

People everywhere, calling, shouting, high-pitched. Should they see a white man, they call, 'Meesta, meesta, how are you?' Polluting human flotsam and jetsam on the river tide and in the streets. Smells, not only spices, but also of putrid waste, discarded, litters the ground at every turn. No Indonesian seems to care, few have any civic pride.

Our children however did not seem to mind, anywhere was preferable to damp, cold England.

Not that Samarinda basks in sunshine for it was built on the banks of the river Makaham, hedged on three sides by jungle and swamp. Mist drifts in from the river early morning and lingers until such time as the sun bursts through and disperses the haze, chokingly mixed with fumes from mini buses, cars and road hogging motorcycles, kerosene powered.

It was a logging town, now more of a trading port and, importantly, the provincial capital of East Kalimantan. Built to last with little planning or thought, a utility; at the same time the centre of government.

Few tourists visit Samarinda and if they do they seldom stay, for they come to visit the hinterland, the Dayak longhouses and old settlements of a bygone era and of course to seek out antiques, especially Chinese porcelain from previous settler dynasties.

*****

Our home is modern and roomy, not unattractive, with a courtyard in which we place a scraggly branch of a Casuarina tree to serve as a Christmas tree. We try to make the house look festive and decorate the rooms with Chinese hangings and lanterns. Although the decorations are not the best, our Javanese cook prepares the most sumptuous banquet of dishes which we attack with relish and which delight the senses. All of us love Indonesian food, such a variety of spices used to bring out the flavours; a million different dishes which never seem to satisfy. Always we want to eat more and more.

*****

The next day we speed up to Muara Wahau by speedboat, stopping on the Equator to feast on prawns and fish. The river is in full spate for the monsoon season has arrived and in the narrows of the river we manoeuvre forward in spurts as the boatmen negotiate the rapids. Angling from one swirling backwater to another, avoiding the full force of the churning flow.

The journey takes longer than usual but by late afternoon we arrive at the village, where we clamber ashore, wading through mud, faeces

Negotiating the rapids on the way to Muara Wahau

and debris to where our vehicle awaits us.

It begins to rain, again, as we slither along the logging roads. Either side, the forest looms large and grand with feathery wisps of mist lingering between the branches as the warm moist air mingles with the cooler air drawn in by the rain.

Although the scheme is not far, it seems to take us ages and we are relieved when the first clearings come into sight. Our house is built entirely of timber, no glass, wooden shingles for the roof, floors natural and polished. It is cool during the midday heat, with the roof shingles reflecting the sun's rays.

We tour the schemes and visit the village of Muara Wahau and attend the numerous Dayak celebrations and festivities which these smiling and contended people seemed continuously to be happily involved with.

Crowds stroll about the longhouse village. How our children loathe being poked, patted, stared at, their hair stroked and their skin admired for being so white and creamy. We are followed everywhere by the villagers. Their smiling, gentle, countenances, pale complexions, a slight blush lightens up their untanned faces, for the forest they inhabit shades them from the fierce tropical sun above.

*****

I was asked by GTZ, who were operating in the vicinity, if I would inspect a small agricultural scheme they had established to provide a venue for Dayaks to learn about new crops and husbandry techniques.

The scheme was downstream, along a tributary of the river Telan. It was a fascinating trip for the children, for the longhouses close to where the scheme was sited happened to be original in structure, authentic, built partially over the river which provided a pleasant moist coolness.

We come alongside a small shop to buy coconuts to assuage our thirst and then notice an old lady weaving floor mats out of narrow thin slivers of bamboo. The mats are beautifully interwoven; subtle colours extracted from forest plants enhance the decorative style, which we feel would provide warmth and an attractive blend when laid upon our wood panelled floors.

We chatter while seated on the floor of her house, looking out at the murky, full river which meanders slowly by. She serves Julia and me tea, while the children sit on the edge of her veranda dangling their feet in the river. An elderly man arrives and sits down.

He tells us, as a younger woman enters. 'She is my new wife, and she is my first wife,' he says, smiling at the old lady pouring tea. 'She is very old now,' he continues, 'and no longer fun. So that is why I have found a new young wife, which is a blessing,' he adds, 'the spirits have been kind to me.'

All three seem content with this obviously pleasant social arrangement, with no stigma attached to the older lady who is apparently past her best at satisfying the old man.

Julia meanwhile was deliberating over the fact that they seemed perfectly happy together as a family in the same longhouse. 'I wonder what makes him attractive,' asked Julia quietly to herself, 'it must be the long earlobes,' which indeed stretched down a distance, dangling against his chin.

'I cannot imagine this kind of relationship being acceptable in suburban England,' Julia said, as we later speed away from the long house.

'How very civilised; up this muddy tributary, far away from the so called liberal morality of our refined modern state of social awareness, such a relationship just would not survive in a semi-detached in Orpington. Here, it is forged together without rancour and without demeaning either party.'

'Indeed very advanced,' echoed Julia, 'especially enjoyable for the man,' she said, as we approached the long slow ascent through the rapids' surging water and back to Muara Wahau.

*****

The Christmas holidays were soon over and the children and I decided to return by sea from Sangkurilang to Bontang, a coal mining township, and then on to Samarinda by road.

Julia, instead, returned directly to Samarinda by speedboat to confirm airline tickets for herself and the children's return journey and to book tickets from Samarinda to Balikpapan where a connection to Singapore departed twice weekly.

Our trek to Sangkurilang was uneventful and we boarded a sampan (a small boat) to take us to Bontang.

It was a warm sunny day and we steamed pleasantly through a deep green and sparkling sea. After sailing for about forty-five minutes the boat's engine began to sound less rhythmical, steam rose from the engine, which all of a sudden died, the propeller emitting dying gasps and rasps before fading.

The driver looked perturbed.

'It's the cooling system,' he told me, 'I will have to repair it.'

The sun was high, we had drinking water, there was nothing to do but wait under the shade of the boat's canopy.

'If you swim,' I told Rebecca, Rachel and Frank, 'the sea will keep you cool and it will be more pleasant than sitting here.' Embarrassed they shook off their clothes and dived in, trusting the driver was not watching.

Meanwhile the driver had opened the cooling system and found a cracked hose pipe.

'I will have to get a tow,' he told me, 'I have no spare on board.'

The sun rose higher, the children swam, I also dove in and the driver sat in the bow looking for another boat, which he hoped would come to our aid.

Time went slowly by and then in the far distance a sampan was seen. The driver stood up and waved his shirt. We were spotted and our rescuer changed course to our direction.

It was very late when we arrived at Bontang. Fortunately our vehicle was there plus driver, waiting anxiously, hoping that we would arrive before dark, for the journey from Bontang to Samarinda took another two hours and the road was winding and narrow.

However by nine o'clock we arrived in Samarinda and drove to the house. Julia was very relieved to see us.

*****

Cooling off near Bontang

There were no convenient flights from Samarinda to Balikpapan, so we drove to Balikpapan airport to catch the flight to Singapore. When we arrived, to our consternation, the gates were closed.

'You are late,' said the check-in counter clerk.

'No we are not, our ticket says take off 17:00 hrs and it is now 16:15, let us on immediately or I will call the airport manager and security.'

The clerk was reluctant to back down, but I spoke Indonesian and white men speaking Indonesian meant plantation or timber companies or government development schemes and that could mean trouble if there were complaints.

The children's and Julia's tickets were processed grumpily and we walked hurriedly to the departure gate. The gate was closed.

'All passengers have embarked,' I was told.

'No they haven't look, they are still entering the plane.'

Julia blazed her way through the gate, followed by Rebecca, Rachel and Frank, me also, although as a spectator. Officials scurried, the cabin crew looked down at our small party, and beckoned for Julia and tribe to come up. We said our farewells, amongst the perspiring ground crew, and once Julia and the children were safely aboard and the aeroplane's doors closed, I left the tarmac and sauntered back to the airport.

Air travel in distant places can be exceedingly fraught sometimes.

29

How Not to Renew a Contract

My contract was due to be renewed. The Jakarta office of the consultancy firm was awaiting confirmation from the Ministries of Immigration and Employment concerning its approval.

PTP VI had no objection; the World Bank approved because I had just completed their feasibility study, free of charge, as to whether or not shipping coconuts to Samarinda by barge was a viable proposition.

The stumbling block, as always, was the Department of Immigration, which had to be persuaded to pass approval for an expatriate to be employed. Companies were requested to pay for the service, which even then was not automatic, and at the same time they had to continue paying the consultant his fee, while waiting for his contract to be signed.

This continual, exhausting outflow of funds was debilitating, for few companies could afford the outlay of maintaining a consultant without assured reimbursement effected by the donor. And that assurance could not always be guaranteed.

My employer had six consultants with contracts ready for renewal. One was over a year old and the company waited feverishly for his contract to be approved.

It was not easy for such companies, in those days, to survive without considerable backing. Some of the Asian-based companies did receive assistance from various quarters, often from their governments, which allowed them to negotiate from a position of strength.

*****

Meanwhile, back at Muara Wahau I had been joined by my sister-in-law, Frances Banham, while Sir John Banham, her husband, Director General of the CBI, was busy promoting British business in the Far East. She enjoyed the remoteness of the schemes and soon melted into a way of life so opposite to her existence in England.

We toured the schemes and chased wild boar down logging tracks and of course to prevent the ever-present threat of dehydration consumed copious quantities of beer.

Our daily routine was interrupted by the sudden appearance out of the forest of an Englishman on a motorcycle; he was managing a large new oil palm plantation upriver.

He was pleasant, good-humoured and eccentric and, being in need of company, had come to Muara Wahau to relieve his solitude. At the same time he was also hoping to get a lift to Samarinda and his HQ, should there be a seat available on a plane or a boat.

I had arranged for Frances' return trip to Samarinda and then on to Jakarta with a Catholic mission plane which would give her a lift back during its routine visit to Muara Wahau. However, owing to storms and heavy dense cloud cover, the plane was not to be seen.

Frances meanwhile was into her third book and seemed not in the least perturbed that the plane continued to fail to appear.

Then out of the cloud one midday, through a break, the mission plane crept in, landing bumpily on the grass strip. Dayaks ran out from every direction to greet the four passengers and unload the small amount of cargo.

The pilot was in a rush to leave, the weather is not improving, he said. So Frances and our new-found friend hurriedly boarded.

'What about your motorcycle?' I called out.

'Oh leave it. I will pick it up on my return,' came back the answer.

Frances waiting for the missionary plane

I never met him again, although we spoke over the telephone. He lives in France, in the some parish as Piers Groves.

*****

My contract, needless to say, remained unsigned and the company did not want to go on paying me without reimbursement; a difficult position for them, which I well appreciated.

It was therefore agreed that I should leave for the UK to await the renewal of my contract and, once renewed, return again to Samarinda.

I did not come back because while in England I was offered a role

149

in an agricultural development project in Sarawak. When I mentioned this to the Dutch company that I was leaving, they uttered squeals of 'What about your contract with us?'

'Bad luck,' I replied, 'find somebody else. I cannot afford to wait.'

They did not engage anybody else because the Government was now finding it increasingly difficult to recruit the right sort of migrants. Interest had waned.

Likewise, the World Bank no longer wished to continue funding transmigration. The scheme had earned much criticism, often unfairly, but rather like the little old lady who was past her best, so the schemes, after two decades, were now considered to have provided a useful service but were no longer appropriate to the country's needs.

30

Sarawak

Collecting stamps is akin to a geography lesson. When I was young it was a mild obsession, a serious hobby with a huge following of little boys and grown-up men. The-in-between years, rather like ponies for girls before boys captured their attention.

My brother Jonathan and I inherited various stamp collections from grandparents and collected ourselves, which we dutifully handed on to other relatives when we lost interest.

My favourite stamps were those from Sarawak. Colourful and exciting, but usually of little value. A king's head adorned a corner alongside an orang-utan or a Dayak in a feathered head dress. An orchid, a forest glade, a river, all were common scenes depicted on the stamps.

And now I had been asked to join, in this country of head-hunters and spirits, dense jungle and swift flowing rivers, mostly inaccessible and sparsely populated, a project financed by the Canadian Development Agency (CDA) in collaboration with the Malaysian government's planning unit which was attached to the Prime Minister's office.

Fortunately our experience in Kalimantan across the border meant that it would not be a strange or new environment for either myself or Julia.

Both of us were pleasantly surprised on arrival to find the people of Kuching, and the other towns, to be so completely different to those who populated Kalimantan next door.

Kuching, the capital town of Sarawak, was dominated by the

Chinese, sophisticated, urban-dwellers; well-educated, astute, often speaking impeccable English and around whom all business revolved.

The contrast could not have been greater, for none of these qualities could be attributed to the Indonesians of Samarinda and Balikpapan, who although hardworking, tended not to be sophisticated and, except for their expertise in all matters culinary, were more earthy in countenance and manners than their Sarawakian counterparts.

*****

Sarawak had been a fiefdom of an English Devonian family, the Brookes who, in 1835, while holidaying in Singapore and thereabouts, had been called upon by the Sultan of Brunei, who owned Sarawak, to stamp out piracy, control headhunting and subdue the many recalcitrant tribes which continually caused mayhem within his domain.

James Brooke, the best known of the male heirs, mustered an assortment of sailors, adventurers, renegades and loyal natives and, after a series of skirmishes and battles, had by 1838 succeeded in quelling the troublesome tribes and curbing the excesses of the Dayaks, whose head-hunting escapades, guided by the spirits of the forests, were a continual cause of anxiety to the more peaceful members of Sarawakian village society.

The Sultan of Brunei was, needless to say, exceedingly content with James' forceful exertions and suggested that he took over the management of Sarawak, which he agreed to in 1841. Who wouldn't! He thence commenced to reign as the Rajah.

In due course, by 1889, with the aid of the British Royal Navy, which for the past three decades had been charged to making the seas safe around Singapore, Malaya and the China Sea, piracy had virtually came to an end.

*****

The Brookes family ruled wisely, principally by James, until 1868 and then by Charles, who reigned for a further 50 years, then latterly by Vyner until 1946. However to ensure enduring peace and at the same time establish a secure sovereignty midst the troublesome greedy appetites of the major powers in their scramble for colonies, Charles placed Sarawak under British protection in 1888. Thereby enabling the country, under the helm of the patriarchal rule of the Raj, to start trading and developing, as were other lands in that diverse archipelago of states and islands which surrounded them, all of whom were advancing rapidly in respect to their economies.

The people of all tribes, principally the Dayaks, Kadezans, Kelabit, Melanau, Kayans and Muruts the Malays and, of course, the Chinese, were generally content to have a ruler who was neither corrupt nor omnipotent, for much of the power still rested in the hands of the various chiefs who the Raj deliberately supported to ensure a diverse spirit of autonomy, instead of a corrupt, ruthless, omnipotent oligarchy of officialdom, which would otherwise have probably emerged.

*****

The legacies of the Brookes family were many, particularly concerning education, behaviour, tribal harmony and gentleness of habit. The native people were cultivated and mannerly, whether from the remote regions of the country or from the towns.

The Chinese traded with the natives in the interior for timber and jungle produce. Both peoples needed each other; neither could survive without fraternal coexistence. In consequence harmonious relationships within the differing tribal groupings, until this day, still remain strong.

The most important issue however was land; a subject which, worldwide, can be a major bone of contention, an issue which, along with religion, has been the a principal cause of wars throughout the ages. Who owns what and is it worth fighting over?

In Sarawak the Raj ensured that land ownership was fair and

equable; that it belonged to the people for the benefit of the people. This meant that only they, if they so wished, could sell or dispose of the land which they owned or resided upon.

The government refused to interfere in land issues, and this still remained a sticking point for development in the 1990s. I met this major constraint to agricultural advancement many times during my two year stint in Sarawak.

The land issues indeed were very much cause for concern. They ignited fierce debate. Although admirable in principal, the difficulty of procuring land by foreign and native entrepreneurs meant that large scale development was limited. Thus for a plantation company to gain access, required patient and protracted negotiations until every single member of all the families concerned, within the tribe, had agreed to the land's disposal. And that indeed was very infrequent.

31

Union with Malaya

The end of the Rajah Brookes reign came abruptly after World War II when Vyner Brookes ceded Sarawak to Britain in 1946.

The British returning after the war as victors soon realised that their colonies were no longer inhabited by submissive natives, but unlike the French and Dutch, understood that the winds were changing course and a commonwealth of nations was the future instead of persevering with total domination.

India became independent in 1947. Malaya wanted the same but waited until 1957. Burma was independent, while Singapore, frightened of being dominated by Malaya, waited until 1965 before becoming an independent republic. Sri Lanka already had broken the ties of colonialism in 1948.

As for Sarawak, the country was bankrupt after the war. Accountancy had not been the Raj's strong point and Vyner was much criticised for his negligence. The infrastructure over the years also had been sadly neglected, although happiness and contentment thrived within the tribes. However across the border separating Sarawak with Kalimantan, avarice glinted in Indonesian eyes. Sarawak and Sabah were morsels ready to be devoured. They had resources and were about to enter a powerful regional union with the Federated States of Malaya and Singapore, which Indonesia feared would upset the balance of power in the region.

The British, who were now handling all matters of government,

155

realised that Sarawak in the 1960s could not survive as an independent sovereign nation, even though the country's potential remained untapped.

The population was too small, hardly half a million souls, compared to Indonesian's one hundred and fifty million, a seething mass of turbulence. The Dutch had been kicked out, a despot, Bapak Soekarno, was in charge. Chronic poverty amongst an ill-educated population of agrarian peasants had stultified all their hopes and ambitions. They were mere serfs.

Britain also wanted to divest itself of its foreign domains. The country was tired and in debt to the Americans and, fearing that Sarawak and neighbouring Sabah would be gobbled up, promoted negotiations by which Malaya i.e. the Federated States, would join with Sarawak, Sabah and Singapore to create a unified country known as Malaysia. It had also been hoped that Brunei would join the union, but its Sultan elected to remain outside the alliance.

An agreement was reached between the British government and Tunku Abdul Rahman, the Prime Minister of Malaya, by which Malaysia would come into effect in July 1963, although eventually the union was formalised in September.

Meanwhile Indonesia in 1962 was bent on causing strife and war. A rebellion in Brunei had been instigated and encouraged by the Northern Borneo National Army, TNKU, the Indonesian invasion force. Although only a minor skirmish, it indicated that Indonesia was keen on disrupting the formation of Malaysia as a unified mix of states.

The Sultan of Brunei requested assistance from Britain and the rebellion was quickly stamped out. But Indonesia was eyeing up Malaysia as well and had decided that this newly formed nation could easily be taken by force for it was supposed that the Malays would surely side with their Islamic brethren, the Indonesians, when confronted with such a choice.

*****

I remember well the beginning of confrontation in 1964 as I was in Malaysia on Dusun Durian estate, located in the State of Selangor, by the sea, awaiting the Indonesian army to arrive, ready to thwart their attempted landings, revolver in hand.

Needless to say those who did invade the country were repelled. Not only by me on the beach, but also by Mrs. Lawrence of Sungei Sedu estate further down the coast, who captured an elite unit of paratroopers in the act of parachuting down into her prized new rubber plantings. Her anger knew no bounds and the event is recounted in Fading Pictures (same author).

Of course the armies of Britain and Malaya (a predominantly Muslim force) also assisted me and Mrs. Lawrence and continued to provide a pivotal role in ensuring Malaysia's safety. And, coupled with the determination of Tunku Abdul Rahman to consolidate the union of all the States, Indonesia's desire to create a grandiose scheme of regional alignment, axised around Jakarta and therefore Bapak Soekarno, unravelled miserably and chaos enveloped the country. While Malaysia, on the other hand, appeared to become much invigorated by the whole episode; the beginning of a very successful unified mix of different peoples, cultures and languages.

Except that the Singaporean Chinese were not getting on at all well with the Malaysian Malays.

It became increasingly obvious that for the sake of racial harmony Singapore should secede from union with Malaysia. Mr. Lee Kwan Yew, PM of Singapore, was distraught, while Tunku Abdul Rahman, who realised his Malays could never compete with the Chinese, was relieved.

There were many worried faces in Singapore at the time of secession in 1965. Most Chinese were confident of the outcome, while the Malays and Indians felt marginalized. European friends thought

157

that it would not work and of course they were very wrong. Under Prime Minister Mr. Lee Kwan Yew Singapore developed from a sleepy trading post and a strategic base for the British armed forces into a highly modern sophisticated city state much admired around the world.

Meanwhile across the Malacca straits, Bapak Soekarno cheered as the split between Singapore and Malaysia widened, still hoping for a break up of Malaysia by any means. But events were moving too fast, Indonesian soldiers were being outfought in the jungle of Sarawak and a pro-Peking faction, egged on by Mao Tse Tung, ousted Mr. Soekarno, who retired to one of his many palaces.

Top positions in the Indonesian government were taken up by communist supporters who oozed their way into control. Almost immediately anti-Chinese sentiment emerged, aided and abetted by the American CIA, bad luck for the majority of Chinese who were not communists.

A bloody program against the communists was savagely executed by the armed forces and many thousands were exterminated before the blood lust was halted.

Out of the ashes arose a new leader, General Suharto, ably served by Dr. Adam Malik, his Foreign Minister. Both wanted peace and stability and after a series of diplomatic moves confrontation petered out during 1966.

My presence on the beach, revolver to hand, had obviously discouraged any imminent Indonesia invasion, while Mrs. Lawrence's fearsome action against their paratroopers had cooled their appetite for further action.

*****

The Chinese were the losers for they bore the brunt of the purge, although certainly not exclusively. In consequence the Government insidiously commenced a policy of subjugation. The Chinese were forbidden to converse in their own language (in public) or read Chinese literature. Life became exceedingly difficult for them especially in terms of economic survival, and most adopted Indonesian names in order to ingratiate themselves with the new regime, thereby enabling their businesses to survive.

They were also affected socially as young Chinese of both sexes were encouraged to find a spouse from amongst the indigenous population. Even during the 1980s it was noticeable in towns where the Chinese were a small minority that mixed marriages had become most common, through necessity rather than desire.

While the Chinese were being ethnically and culturally watered down, a few steps across the border in Sarawak, life for them continued as before.

It was a legacy promoted by the Raj, adopted by post-war administrations, that the native peoples, including the Chinese and the Malays, whether rural or urban, should be free to live as they wished and in complete harmony with each other.

And, that was how we found life in Sarawak when I commenced my assignment there in 1992.

32

SADP 1992

The Sarawak Agricultural Development Programme (SADP) of 1992, was implemented in order to provide a detailed plan for the future agricultural development of the country.

Agriculture, except for rice growing and the Chinese managed pepper gardens, was generally poorly performed and only on a small scale.

There were exceptions, two plantations had been established by private corporations in central Sarawak close to Bintalu. The Commonwealth Development Corporation (CDC) had planted an oil palm plantation in Miri province and also rattan for furniture, an interesting introduction as an industrial crop.

But generally, as explained before, permission to develop any large-scale commodity crop enterprise was difficult to obtain from the natives who owned the land and, being uninterested in working in an orderly fashion, large-scale schemes, which require a disciplined approach, lacked appeal, while participation in smallholder farming enterprises remained popular.

However across the Kalimantan/Sarawak border Indonesians were queuing up at recruiting centres, and also entering illegally, using hidden paths which snaked through the jungle.

Sarawak, for an Indonesian, was a haven, good salaries, a secure and stable government and a meritocratic system within the commercial world, which offered opportunities and employment to those who wanted to work, and Indonesians were very good workers.

*****

For me, as agronomist (what a splendid title), the idea of becoming involved in small scale agriculture was new but definitely appealing for it embraced not only different cropping systems but also agroforestry, which was becoming a popular inclusion. For every community used the products from the forest, whether the jungle be primary or secondary.

It was therefore essential to look at each topographical zone, coast to mountains, in order to provide practical, economically viable models for adoption by the residing communities. Which meant that I had to visit all the zones to assess the current situation. To complete such models without entering the interior would have been impossible.

33

The Interior

Thus I set off to explore Sarawak. What an exciting and purposeful way of touring a country and what diversity to enjoy.

I visited a wide range of communities, Sea Dayaks, Land Dayaks, Kelabit Kadezans, Malays, Chinese and all the others. Each different in some way or other, whether physically, spiritually, socially or intellectually; a myriad lifestyles and views.

Most of the natives were simple people, although often extraordinarily sophisticated in their social awareness and community spirit. They were hospitable to outsiders, such as myself. I entered briefly into their lives slept in their longhouses, drank their delicious tuak (rice wine) drawn from the previous year's harvest.

We talked of days past, in English, seldom Malay, for many had been educated in English and still held a fondness for the Brookes family and the colonial officers who visited their homes and cultivated plots, slashed and burnt within the forests; to advise and guide, never imposing themselves unduly upon such unassuming gentle people. Patriarchal probably, diligent, sneered at now by modern society, but certainly supportive and effective then, and, still well remembered and appreciated by the native people of the forest.

*****

My arrival would be greeted with interest. Old ladies watched through loose-fitting window shutters, the men-folk seemed genuinely pleased. I would be welcomed into a longhouse, my boat made fast against a swaying pole stuck in the river or tied around a foundation post.

We sat on reed mats and discussed the vagaries of different lifestyles, seldom about the crops they grew, for they would be difficult to sway, although always eager to learn of new opportunities.

The lowland natives grew their rice upon virgin land, on flat or sloping hills, felled, burned and winnowed to provide space. Delicious long-eared rice, seed collected year after year; selected each time and passed down through generations. Hybrids unknown, genetically modified crops a decade away. Enough for the family, wine making and sale; nutritious and abundant, harvested from the same field until fertility declined and the farmer moved on afresh.

I reasoned, 'Please use fertiliser, then you can use the same plot for six years. By this way you will save your forest for generations to come.'

Quiet smiles greet my brief eloquence, shy nods of assent.

'But, that is not what we have done in the past. The jungle will return,' they insist, 'in fifty years' time.'

They think in generations, not minutes or hours like us.

They keep a few pigs and the odd cow. Fruit trees; mangos, breadfruit, passion fruit, mangosteens, rambutans and durian abound. In the districts near Kuching, Samarahan and Sri Aman, rubber is grown and tapped periodically when a festival or celebration is due and urgent funds are needed.

Fish no longer abound in the rivers owing to the adulterated mix of silt in the flowing waters which gets stuck inside their gills. Loggers moving upstream to extract the valuable timber do not understand the despoliation and contamination they cause. A way of life gradually being lost owing to the insatiable greed of man for all things in and under the soil, without thought of the past or the future.

*****

Drinking tuak in a longhouse

The natives knew that this so-called progress would eventually swamp them. However, although most wanted the advantages that modern civilisation had to offer, particularly medicine, consumables, communications and electricity, they could not understand why raping the forests should be the only way of meeting their modest needs.

'Surely,' they asked, 'the government could impose a law allowing only selective thinning of the forest, sufficient to pay for our needs.'

Roads and airports were not what they wanted and definitely developers disturbing their peace were unwelcome.

There was no answer to their questions, selective tree harvesting was the official government policy, but seldom adhered to. 'You cannot have one without the other,' was the usual lame reply. At least there was wine to mellow their worries.

165

'Down the hatch!' one amiable gentleman called.

'Cheers!' shouted another.

'Have you ever been to Hampton Court?' I was asked by a wizened old man with long earlobes stretching to his shoulders, 'I have never been there ...' he said.

I am attentive.

'It's not far from London, you know ...' he continued. I listen. Everybody reveres this old man and all were quiet.

Nobody murmurs or laughs. What could he know about Hampton Court I wonder?

Another sip of wine follows and then another.

'When I went to Buckingham Palace the Queen asked me where I came from. So I told her and she said she would visit my longhouse. This longhouse.'

He waved his arm tremulously encompassing the wooden building.

'She never came, you know.'

Murmurs, sighs from the squatting throng. All in English, they understood.

'But I did go to Ascot, it was the best day of my life.'

He had indeed met the Queen, one of her first visitors after the Coronation. An experience which lingers in his mind and those who live in his longhouse. Sadly he never went to Henry VIII's favourite abode, Hampton Court, although probably his forebears had acted in similar fashion to Henry when getting rid of their enemies in days gone by, for preserved heads often played a prominent part in the décor of a Dayak longhouse.

*****

Sarawak was very much an anomaly. It was the only state in Malaysia where English was more widely spoken than Malay, and also fluently by many. I seldom had to speak in Malay, even my Malay driver always spoke to me in English. The only language which I did continue to use, occasionally, was Tamil, an Indian dialect, for some of the staff in the Governor's office, where we were based, were Tamils. Although throughout Sarawak there were very few Indians. A Brookes' policy, I was told.

They were a forgotten community, a few handfuls dotted about the country, always in towns, Kuching, Miri, Bintalu. They lived together, socially separate, rarely did they integrate with the other Sarawakian ethnic groupings. I would, when passing through the offices, sometimes talk with them, they were pleased to converse with an outsider who could speak their language.

'What should I do?' one asked me, as I was sauntering down a corridor, 'My daughter is fourteen and betrothed to a forty year old man. How can she have sex with him? He is too old and she is too young and small.'

'Limit him,' I replied, 'to once a month, and then increase the number of times as she gets older. And if he disagrees, then tell him the betrothal is off.' 'But he is rich and we are poor,' she sighed, 'we need the money.'

'Then ask the Great Lord Krishna to protect her,' I suggested, as I continued on my way.

'Our Great Lord Krishna has protected us,' she told me a week later.

'Oh, how?' I asked.

'Her husband to be was so overcome with my daughter's beauty that his heart stopped and today he is being cremated,' she answered happily.

A satisfactory ending for the bride, although bad luck for he who had paid the price for a virgin bride, but had not enjoyed the fruits of his purchase.

167

34

The Mountains

Researching my models I travelled to Miri then by an internal flight to Ba Kelahan in the mountains, close to the Kalimantan border, where serious fighting during confrontation had taken place.

The jungle was pristine, for how long one could not tell, but the billowing canopies and huge forest trees swathed the country as far as the eye could see.

The air was clear and cool. Apples grew, not very well. While vegetables and fruits of various kinds abounded. Cattle and goats grazed. A rich variety of produce could be grown here without difficulty, should a transport system be introduced.

In many of the houses only the elderly resided, the younger generation were migrating to the towns, for there was little to hold them here.

I decided to stay a couple of days with the local agricultural officer and then journey on by foot to Bareo. However in between me and Bareo was Gunong (mountain) Murud, almost 8000 ft high. I did not want to go up it and then down the other side. So I took the easy option and decided to cross the border into Kalimantan and march around and then pick up the trail through the foothills thereby bypassing Murud and G. Batu Buli, and then a mere saunter up to Bareo.

*****

I slipped away quietly one early morning across the border and into Kalimantan. The track was well-trodden and after about two hours of marching I stopped off at a village where I sipped coffee with the headman. Here I had to speak Malay as nobody could speak English.

The headman, for a small fee, suggested his son gave me a lift on his motorcycle. This enabled me to continue my onward journey and off we sped along jungle tracks, through streams, over log bridges, passing irrigated rice fields, which the Indonesians managed so well.

Beautifully picturesque, dappled greens and browns, past swift-flowing sparkling, clear streams running through valley bottoms. It was a pleasant journey and by midday we arrived at the border town of Kumering.

I had no passport and only an identification card, which showed my official position and where I was based, the Planning Department of the Governor's office, Kuching, Sarawak. I hoped this would be sufficient should I meet an Indonesian policeman, who no doubt would be mightily disconcerted to bump into a lone Englishman in such an isolated region, so far from officialdom and authority.

*****

As we motorcycled around the outside of the town, hooded, furtive eyes followed our every move. Past wooden thatched houses built on stilts and ugly corrugated-roofed shops we weaved our way, eventually arriving at a small eating house which served the most delicious fried river fish, rice with chilli paste and tips of ferns (paku ikan). Although a very simple meal, in a western restaurant it would have been regarded as being haute cuisine of exotic taste. As the Philippines directed their talent to music, so the culinary art of cooking was very much the culture of Indonesia.

Meanwhile my motorcycle driver negotiated with another to take me on and drop me at the jungle edge for tomorrow's journey to Bareo. He parted, thanking me for the fare and tip, then with my new driver I set off once again.

On the way to Bareo

*****

By late afternoon we arrived at a loseman (rest house) where I was deposited. It was full, but the old lady who managed the house allowed me to stay in the police sergeant's room as he was away on night duty.

I promised to leave at first light, so after an evening meal I slept until awoken by a chorus of birds and chickens as dawn approached.

The old lady was up, making breakfast and lunch for those staying at the rest house. She sat on the floor close to a small fire, surrounded by the ingredients for the forthcoming day's meal.

How composed she was, never moving any part of her body except

171

for her arms and hands, as she kneaded, cut, ground, slapped and cooked the various ingredients. Everything she needed was close to hand, such economy of movement and organisation have I only seen before in fishing boats on rivers, the fishermen hardly moving except for what was essential to their fishing and paddling activities. Never was a movement made without thought and purpose. No energy was wasted under the hot tropical sun.

I drank a cup of sweet tea, paid the old lady and departed hastily. She pointed me in the direction of the mountain path. I was eager to leave before the police sergeant returned from his duties.

*****

It was a long hike up into the mountains. I passed through dense jungle, wondering if I was on the right track. I rested by fast flowing steams and slowly quenched my thirst. Deer barked in the background, pigs ran away with snuffling snorts. Lizards watched me. Sometimes a small party of traders and porters hurried down.

'Why are you alone?' they would call to me. 'It is dangerous, there are wild animals; maybe a bad spirit of the jungle will attack you.'

I always answered, 'Being alone is easier, you can walk at your own speed. Nobody to worry about, but myself.'

'You need a friend,' they would counter, 'should you hurt your leg.'

Company, people, togetherness, was their society and it worked well for them. A community of people walking in the jungle, so unnatural for a solitary figure to be on his own.

By mid-afternoon I was tired and my leg muscles ached. 'I am unfit,' I thought, 'how weedy one becomes being a consultant. Too much sitting, instead of hiking to a village. No longer becoming assimilated with the environment and the rural scene; so important to understand and feel.'

'Well at least I am doing something useful, my models will be true, factual

Resting an the way to Bareo

and actual without using modern technology to provide the substance.'

*****

At last I arrive at the border and sidle into Sarawak, but I still have some distance to go to reach Bareo. Should I rest up and stay the night, I consider. There are small villages close to the path, which is now widening to become a track.

I stop and ask a Kelabit farmer where I can stay. He offers his house. I accept and a wonderful evening unfolds of stories and companionship, delicious rice wine and music, smiling faces.

The revelries seemed to go on all night but eventually I am allowed to sleep. They are not impressed with my physical exertions, for they journey up and down this mountain range every week.

The people, slight and wiry, are mere beasts of burden. The women bear loads of equal weight to the men, while children are always weighed down with smaller parcels.

One feels considerable compassion and sympathy for these poor farmers and traders who march up and down the hills to carry their trade goods and on the return journey bring up supplies. They climb the steep slopes without complaint, using woven pannier baskets, carried as a rucksack, high on their shoulders, a strap over the forehead to support the load.

How could this way of life be changed? This is hardly bus route terrain. Perhaps one should just leave well alone such ethnic vagaries, which from a western viewpoint are so difficult to comprehend.

*****

Everybody is so cheerful, expecting nothing, committed to their lifestyle. Should a western anthropologist try to change it, could he or she promote an alternative way of living? At the same time should not some effort be made to alleviate the burden of these people subsisting in these isolated communities throughout the country? Their jollity and good humour masking the drudgery of their tough existence.

However they did not regard their life as being particularly onerous nor tiresome. It was part of their culture to traverse the mountains and forests heavily laden, seeking out forest products and trading in the valleys below.

How could we help? What model can I conjure up? Anthropologists come and go, always with a solution. A few are worthy, most interested only in claiming a PhD after another exhaustive study of the native tribes of Sarawak.

Their entry into the longhouses was always treated with good humour by the inhabitants, as they asked endless questions in foreign accents, often answered with peals of laughter.

While at Bareo two Dutchmen were collecting facts and figures. They went from longhouse to longhouse and eventually arrived at the one I happened to be in. Tall and angular, all knobs and knees, they spread themselves on the matted floor.

The headman greeted them graciously and asked, which part of England did they come from.

'We come from Holland,' they replied. There was quietness.

'Then it must be near London,' the old man quietly surmised.

'No, no,' said one of the Dutchman, 'no, no, not England, Holland.' he said loudly, exasperated. 'Another country,' reaffirming his allegiance to Holland.

'Holland, England, it is the same,' came the gentle response, 'you see I can hear your voice, it is just like that of a soldier in the British Army, a cockney's.' Peals of laughter reverberated around the wooden longhouse.

'I know,' he exclaimed exuberantly, 'I was a scout with the Tommies during confrontation when they were fighting the Indonesians, I know the accent.' I joined in the merriment, wine, laughter and a joke were loved by all.

*****

Bareo village nestled comfortably on a plateau surrounded by mountains and dense jungle. Scudding clouds and fingers of wispy mist cloaked the forest. In the centre a grass airstrip provided limited access, where planes from Miri unloaded consumables and loaded on products from the land.

Upland rice was grown under irrigation, bamboo pipes brought water down from hillside springs to feed the crop. Fruits and vegetables were grown but insufficient for commercial sale. My models would have to dwell on how the villagers should try to make a living off the land by selling their produce in the towns beyond the mountain range.

And tourism, of a specialist nature, could be encouraged. Few tourists ever visited, although the majestic scenery was enticing, the climate pleasant and the people convivial. Walks in the jungle to view the birds and rare butterflies would provide an interesting opportunity to those wishing to immerse themselves in the beauty of unspoilt jungle. Of which, unhappily, so little is left worldwide.

35

The Plan

A plan for the future development of this slice of Borneo was fashioned. Doug Webster, a Canadian Professor, drafted and Karl Kuchera, a Cartographer, mapped the areas involved, while David Woodward, a Russian-speaking Economist, (who I still meet) helped with the economic details and was the only person in our team able to combat the local Chinese Economist, who inhabited the agricultural department and whose ferocity could be quite unnerving.

Eventually to quieten him down, I threatened that Julia, having been born in Cornwall and knowing the witches' jargon and the power of the ley lines worshipped by the Druids, would cast a spell on him. Although Chinese, he was Sarawakian, and believed in spells and sorcery.

It was astonishing that the threat worked and he did quieten down considerably, passing, at the same time, an evil eye upon me, should I be present at a meeting that he was attending.

*****

When the draft was presented, it was not what they wanted. They were jubilant, 'This is inadequate, where are the places?... the facts? ... the figures?' they squealed. 'More detail please, all costs related, tabulated, times, dates when the programme should be implemented.'

It was not to be just a guide, they argued, the plan had to be designed for implementation; all sequences of development to encompass every zone.

'An impossible task to undertake in a two year period,' we countered. 'Extend the period of time,' they suggested.

'Can't,' said the Canadian Diplomat drawn into the meeting, 'our budget is sufficient for two years only.'

We had a meeting with the Central Economic Planning Unit in the Prime Minister's department, Kuala Lumpur, and thrashed out a further input and a compromise was reached.

My smallholder farming systems, still uncompleted, began to take shape; they were an essential ingredient to the plan. Doug Webster laboured away trying to ensure coherence and objectivity to a plan which was becoming more and more detailed as time went on. It was not easy.

36

Music and the Hash House Harriers (HHH)

Julia entered a thriving music scene. At her first recital, for which she had not prepared before performing as assiduously as usual, suddenly found out that half of the Chinese performers had either graduated from London's Royal Academy or the Royal College of Music or from the Northern School of Music. Nearly all the audience were Chinese and had come to provide a critical ear to her playing.

Classical music was very much a legacy of the last Rannie Brookes, Sylvia, wife of Vyner. She was herself a pianist of some repute and would often hold soirees in Kuching's central park at a pavilion built where musicians could play at the weekend.

Julia's performance was well-received and the Sarawak music scene broached. (Many of the teachers and musicians have remained firm friends over the years, particularly June Lin and her family).

*****

The British Council also thrived and for many years organised, with the assistance of the Sarawak Music Society, the import of soloists, quintets, bands, singers and dancers to perform in the main towns of the country. It was very popular, providing culture and, just as important, good will.

Unfortunately, the British government decided the Council, owing to financial constraints, should bring the musical and artistic extravaganza to an end, resulting sadly in the Council becoming merely an institution of learning and libraries only. Culture was out and extra-curricular activities became a thing of the past.

It was so disappointing for those many, from all walks of life, who enjoyed music, whether jazz or classical. Suddenly Sarawak became bereft of visiting musicians, the legacy of the Rannie was over. Sad for everybody and especially those living in the smaller and more isolated communities of Sarawak where the musicians had been asked to perform during their visit.

The support had gone and the British Council in Kuching appeared totally unconcerned with the decision and even supported it. But they were only civil servants, mere conduits of the government's policy of cost cutting.

*****

Not so the Hash House Harriers, a band of weekly runners who followed paper trails up and down dale laid by a human hare. Villagers were amused with our antics invariably mimicking the distant calls of 'On, on' when the trail was found after being lost or changed. The runs laid through village, jungle and swamp, over streams and rivers, were immensely popular and enjoyed by all who turned up week after week.

It became an addiction for us. Even Julia who never considered herself a cross-country athlete enjoyed the chase.

Frank at eleven years old, fit and keen from school in England, ran effortlessly with the leaders and became known as 'The Bullet' for he always returned with the leading runners. Tireless, hardly panting, while I was nearly always last; taking clever short cuts, which were not, and thereby getting lost. On one occasion arriving back at 7.00 p.m.

The girls ran, panting and puffing, wondering how much further they had to endure.

At the finishing point, we stumbled in breathless and exhausted. Visiting runners, journeying through Sarawak, would say the Kuching HHH was the hardest they had ever experienced and, certainly

Frank leading the HHH pack

compared to runs organised in West Malaysia, they were indeed set over the most difficult of terrain.

Beer and soft drinks were quaffed in gallons at the end of the run. For at least an hour Julia and I could barely move or speak; Frank probably could have run another.

In the evening there was the 'On On', a weekly celebration to our fitness and resolve. It was great fun; a cross-section of Sarawak society enjoying a convivial evening out after an exhausting afternoon. We ate delicious Chinese food and drank more beer, all to ooze out later in the week when we set off again on an HHH run.

Although there were less than twenty Europeans in Kuching, half would join the fray. Most of the runners were Chinese, at least 40, with the reminder being Dayaks or Kadezans. Only occasionally would a Malay run.

It was great entertainment and each week we all looked forward to the Saturday Hash and sometimes the midweek chase as well, although this was only for males, being much more difficult than the Saturday run when both sexes took part.

*****

Unfortunately our time in Sarawak was drawing to a close. My contract period neared conclusion. Although both Julia and I would have loved to have stayed on, most of the consultants had already departed and only the chief of project staff, plus David Woodward, Karl Kuchera and myself remained. Jackie Wong, an Economist from Malaysia, had come to assist and became a firm but distant friend.

Doug Webster left the project, his input deflated after having a tiff with his wife, the result of which precluded any further involvement. David W. remained a little longer then went to Russia, while Karl joined another mapping project in Sarawak.

I packed my bags for Papua New Guinea (PNG) where I was to promote similar models for the government. PNG turned out to be a very dissimilar country indeed compared to Sarawak.

37

PNG and the Rascals

During the next one and a half years, 1993 and 1994, I visited PNG twice. My first visit was made to appraise the various tree crop research institutions in order to ascertain how funds provided by external donors were being utilised. Was the money being effectively spent in the way it should have been? Was research being adequately funded? Request you recommend any appropriate new programmes that would be beneficial. Resources, detail requirements for the following years budget, please.

*****

My first trip was to the Highlands to the Coffee Research Station at Goroka, high up in the Bismarck range. It was cold at night and cool during the day even when the sun pierced the hanging cloud.

There was an aura of menace. The Highlanders, as they were referred to, were rough, tough, often violent, people. Recently a policeman had been killed in a brawl; in consequence the police took revenge by burning down villages inhabited by the villains, who were referred to as the 'rascals', a delightful name which all wrong-doers were labelled.

Needless to say this resulted in further killings and burnings, carried out by both sides. The Highlands was not a safe place and roadblocks were frequent and mounted by attentive fierce-looking police.

However it was not only in the Highlands where violence was

endemic, Port Moresby, the capital, once the sun had retired for the night, was also a dangerous place, where muggings and robbery were perpetrated frequently. Sometimes just outside the gates of houses and apartments such as ours, not in the sleazy suburbs of town but in the more salubrious areas of downtown Port Moresby. And not only at night.

Daytime break-ins, rape and general mayhem were not infrequent, as I experienced one Sunday afternoon. Julia had returned to the UK, having decided that three weeks in PNG was enough to last her a lifetime, when there was a polite knock on my apartment door. I opened it to behold a gang of rascals holding machetes, knives and spears. My apartment was in a complex, with brave guards recruited to safeguard our welfare from villainous intruders, but lo and behold on my doorstep stood six ruffians, all well-armed.

'Good afternoon,' I greeted them. They replied, the same. 'Can I help you?' I asked politely.

'We come lookem big fellah lawyer, he live along here, which house belong him?'

Indeed the Attorney General lived next door to us. An Australian, he seemed a nice person, quiet and unassuming, I was glad he wasn't here now.

'I am afraid he has returned to Aussie. Him go forever,' I told them.

A look of disappointment clouded their terrifyingly aggressive faces, huge noses a quivering.

'I don't know when him return, probably never,' I continued. 'Why do you want to fight this big fellah lawyer?' I asked.

'Him hang brother belong me,' replied one, 'now I findem and killem.' 'What did your brother do?' I asked the rascal. 'Him must have been plenty bad man to hang.'

Capital punishment was still in vogue in PNG.

The rascal band looked at each other, then conspiratorially, the

184

victim's brother learned forward and whispered 'He killem fellah in brawl, fight fair and dinkum; me savvy he drink too much, but fight good one and true. Judge say, my brother bad too much, you die, finish. So brother belong me now dead. Judge him must die to, this time now, me stickem good.'

I felt very relieved I was not a member of the PNG judiciary.

'Well I am very sorry indeed about your brother, but Judge him gone along now, so best you go back home side and look after your missus and piccaninny.'

How do I get rid of them? I wondered, or they might just stickem me instead. An alternative objective which should appeal to their violent natures was required. Of course, ideal, just the job, I thought, for up on the hill above the apartment nestled the houses of various Ambassadors, High Commissioners, Heads of the IMF, World Bank, NGO's and others. Port Moresby's society in abundance, all of whom would benefit from a good hiding by an irate bunch of rascals on a Sunday afternoon.

I escorted the rascals as nonchalantly as possible to the gate, where our worthy guards were still not to be seen and all the apartments appeared empty of residents. 'Up there plenty big fellah stop along, you want to bang up big fellahs you go up there, plenty living up along hill,' I coaxed them in the direction, pointing to the houses above. They seemed pleased to be part of a scheme, which would allow them to vent their anger. Hopefully those up there had braver guards than ours down here.

I felt rather relieved to have got rid of the gang so quickly. Although I realised robbing and pillaging an Ambassador's lodging would probably be considered, in polite circles, inappropriate behaviour.

Anyway, better than assaulting me, consultant to ANZDEC Ltd., son of Babs Bryant of Cambridge University, Soccer Blue and friend of the Tribal Chief of Baluchistan.

*****

In the evenings it was not wise to travel unless in a fast car with the windows closed. Having been cannibals not so long ago, the New Guineans' violent tendencies lay just below the surface. Once, in a respectable pub downtown, a middle class gent in a suit, although ill-fitting, grabbed his wife's hair, or possibly it could have been his girlfriend's and hurled her across the bar and then heaved the lady through the door. This melee drew no snorts of disapproval or condemnation; it was obviously the way differences were settled in smart society. If your missus misbehaved she was dealt with in a truly physical fashion. Such behaviour, dominant and aggressive, had been passed down through the ages.

When journeying to Irian Jaya on one occasion, a lingering memory of uncivilised behaviour occurred while I awaited my turn at the check-in-counter in the airport; suddenly a mob converged on a Papuan, who was also checking in at the same time, and hustled him away through the glass doors separating the outside world from the departing customers. However, only a step outside they were confronted by an equally terrifying mob, the Papuan's friends, plus the police, who hurled themselves into the melee.

My check-in-lady was completely unfazed.

'Him small fight between clans,' she acknowledged, as twirling truncheons, fists and cudgels banged down on heads. 'Thank you for travelling Air Nuiginea,' the counter lady said, smiling, as she handed me my boarding card, 'have a safe flight.'

I blinked at the mayhem outside and sauntered through to the departure lounge.

38

Collingwood Bay and Kokoda

During my second visit Julia stayed on to see the country before returning to England. She exulted in the scenery and climate of PNG but found little else to empathise with.

We visited the two project sites at Collingwood Bay on the east coast and Kokoda district inland, where there had been fierce fighting during World War II between the Australians and the Japanese.

Over the years an amicable affinity coexisted between the Aussies and the Papuans. They got on remarkably well, both having forceful, turbulent characters. They mixed freely, for neither side had a retiring disposition and a physical, non-intellectual relationship welded them together in a fitful but generally loyal friendship.

The country for all its unruliness was a happy place, lots of laughs and slapstick, nobody seemed to work very hard. Although the Islanders were much more industrious than the people of the Solomons, their neighbours, who were regarded as being generally slothful, feeble but tasty, a good meal enjoyed by all, a few decades back.

*****

Collingwood Bay, in the district of Wanigella was picturesque and we were joined by an entomologist who was determining the effect that any proposed development might have upon the local butterfly population, particularly the habitat of the rare Queen Alexandra, which one was occasionally lucky to espy, quivering silently amidst the trees and flowering shrubs of the villages. It was indeed a very beautiful, large and glamorous species and certainly more pleasant of character than the Cassowary bird who the villagers used as guard dogs. Spiteful and bitter they would launch themselves at you should you approach, neck outstretched beak to the fore. Definitely not a creature to spar with.

We stayed in the village of Wanigella and surveyed the bay and its picturesque villages. We scrambled through mangrove, over seashores, into the land beyond the sea, where sago palms provided sustenance and rattan grew densely in the villager's gardens, climbing up into the forest canopies high above. The villagers lived off fish and sago flour, but they wanted to earn more money. A small cottage industry of bark paintings existed which were sent to Port Moresby for sale. A handful of the more progressive and literate farmers were starting to process end products from their crops. One had produced a very drinkable strong coffee from his own Robusta bushes, and another, a sour chocolate into which I suggested a small mix of sugar would enhance the taste.

Agroforestry opportunities existed, for a rich cradle of plant life covered the landscape throughout this coastal district. It was a paradise. Daily, sudden drenching rains would, like a blanket, sweep down the coast, swirling past in deluges leaving behind a misty glow as the sun peeped through the damp cloudy air. In such a hothouse environment every tropical crop would luxuriate.

As the models took shape, rattan cultivation, based on the experience of CDC in Sarawak, would be well-suited to Collingwood Bay and had considerable economic potential. Also pepper, spices, patchouli, the aromatic tree ylang ylang, plus other essential oils, fruits and nuts. This district could support a whole range of exotica.

*****

After a few weeks in the project area Julia and I returned to PNG to build up our hungry frames, gorging ourselves on pizzas and pies, the standard fare, before returning to the field. Both of us found the food in the villages distinctly unappetising. While our colleagues scoffed heartily, we picked delicately, trying not to cause offence by showing our total dislike for the dishes presented before us, even the rice was indescribable both in taste and texture. It was no different in Kokoda.

We drove to Kokoda from Port Moresby with a small escort of extension officers who were thoroughly agitated to be leaving their secure government offices and certainly were not relishing the task of discussing crop issues with the rascals who, similar to the Italian Mafia, appeared to control village life in the district, when not trying to spear each other or hapless government officers who came to mediate over their differences. We, however, found them most pleasant people who enthusiastically offered suggestions concerning which crops would suit their communities, rubber and cocoa being particularly popular.

In the evenings Julia and I bathed in icy, clear tumbling rivers, to wash off the day's sweat and dirt. It was exhilarating and refreshing to be soaping ourselves in spotless clean water. Ready for another day, although often hungry, but that did not matter, and Julia became as slim as she had ever been. Primitive culinary practices an adopted diet of sago biscuits, just eatable, vegetables cooked in coconut oil and cloggy, watery rice, a spoonful at a time, inhibited our eating habits. And, if available, a bottle of beer cooled in a stream, helped stem our hunger.

*****

Our recommendations were received with optimism by the Ministry of Agriculture in Port Moresby and, it was hoped, they would be pushed fast forward and implemented. Fortunately there were a number of Australians and enthusiastic locals in the Ministry eager to support our proposals.

It was always disappointing when advice and suggestions were slow to be employed. Very often one spent two to three months exploring opportunities for smallholders to adopt only to find that the

189

institutions earmarked to provide the support were either not available or too busy on other matters.

And yet so little assistance is needed for a farmer, keen, willing and energetic, to put into effect an agricultural recommendation, provided he is able to buy or procure the planting material and learn the basic husbandry practices, which any local trained agricultural officer should be able to supply.

*****

The report and models are to be edited and finalised in New Zealand, my contract ends and I make my last departure out of PNG.

I say goodbye to the local staff who are now returning to their own offices in the Ministry of Agriculture. I pack and leave the key of my apartment with the agency in downtown Port Moresby.

I call a taxi and, with my two small bags, ask the driver to take me to the airport.

'I have to buy some fuel first,' he says, and we stop at a petrol station.

My eyes wander to a TV in the window of an adjacent store. An advertisement is being shown, a happy family group eating spam.

'Why does the TV station advertise spam?' I ask the driver, 'everybody eats spam here, it hardly needs advertising.'

The driver thinks long and hard and says, 'All one talk Iikem spam because him taste like pig.'

Quiet follows, then, 'Pig him good too much, pig him like meat belong you and me.'

So the taste buds remain the same after many decades, a cut of succulent bottom, if allowed, would still be the best meat in town.

Stella

39

A Detour

In 1994 I found myself in Tanzania again. Simon Mbollo met me at the airport and we drove to Kunduchi and up to the Mantheakis farm.

It was now four years since I had previously been on one of my yearly excursions to visit NCDP operations, which unfortunately had suffered a reversal of fortune; drought, pestilence and disease had affected the hybrid's survival rate and the project had been downgraded accordingly by GTZ. Funds were reduced considerably.

Dogs greeted me, cautiously, surrounding the car as we drew up, sniffing, seeking to discover my identity. Nothing seemed to have changed, although the garden surrounding Stella's house, once ours, now seemed more luxuriant than before, with many varieties of new flowering plants growing prolifically amongst the ylang ylang trees, mangoes and oranges.

I opened the veranda door and entered.

'Hodi, hodi?' I called out (May I come in?)

Quiet reigned throughout; no sounds stirred the calm cool interior of the home. The doors were open and I glimpsed inside. Changed from our day, paintings, artwork, books, a home, the high ceilings arching shadows in the light, a sense of spaciousness. Expressing that hint of grandeur.

I walk around, through the kitchen, onto the veranda again, where we used to sit as a family at a long dining table, still there. My reverie is suddenly broached by a wild screech. My first thought is pain, somebody, some animal, I look around, hesitant, and grip the back of a chair ready to use it in my defence should I be attacked by a raving lunatic or prowling jackal.

Another piercing screech, 'Hodi hodi!' followed by a cackle of laughter.

I wince, and search around furtively and then glimpse the source of my fear, a parrot, such a human voice coming from so colourful a bird.

From the other side of the veranda another voice, another call, more human, but not yet distinguishable; who is that? definitely not another parrot, I surmise, definitely human.

'It is me, Robin,' I call back.

'Robin, Robin, Robin!' A piercing cry, it is Stella's voice. 'I saw in the cards that you were returning to Tanzania!'

She bustles around a corner, a flowing figure, towards me. We embrace. She seeks confirmation that her card reading has been true and accurate from a trailing Michael, who works both for Stella and her younger son Michel at his safari camps. He nods that indeed he also knew of my pending arrival. Oscaria too, the housemaid, also joins in this chorus of affirmatives.

'Come ...' she says to me, and we return together from whence she had emerged.

The whole of this side of the veranda houses a mass of bones, roots, branches and stones. On a workbench her decorative artwork lies awaiting the final detail from her dextrous and artistic touches.

Her work is imaginative and alive. A root is turned into a candle mounting, a boat from an improbable piece of old bone; stars flutter from sprigs of dried moss.

'Look,' she says, 'what do you see?' Excited, demanding to get my opinion.

'I see a mass of spindly roots, without either shape or form,' I answer.

'Aren't they beautiful,' she ignores my utterances, 'look at them closely.' She turns a root upside down. 'Isn't it striking,' she continues 'think of a colour which will highlight and enhance its shape and form and bring it alive. Can't you see Robin? I thought you had some imagination!'

'I have,' I reply, 'in abundance.'

But unfortunately it precludes artwork, which was never a strong subject during my scholarly years.

She is disappointed that I cannot see a bright Christmas decoration in a tangled piece of dried branch. Her thoughts and feelings run riot as she shows me her work, so easy to appreciate once completed but hard to discern when nothing but a withered stick or dried vegetable lies waiting to be transformed.

'Let's celebrate your return. Come ...' and I follow her around to the other side of the house.

'Michael, bring the vodka, ice, lots of it.' The parrot quizzes me with her round alert eyes, 'Robin! Robin!' she squawks. A quick learner I think to myself, what next?

*****

Indeed, what will this house of a thousand memories yield to me over the next few days? We talk non-stop; what am I doing here, are you staying, where are you living, working, playing? We explore our lives.

'My life,' she interrupts me, 'is indescribable, it is a pottage of thwarted ambition. My life is without order.' A long sigh follows. This is accompanied by a gesture of sublime resignation. So beautifully Greek, fatalistic and dramatic.

She interrupts herself, 'Michael call the boys, tell them Robin has come back.'

Being dutiful sons they will probably come quickly as bidden.

*****

Michel is hunting and is betrothed to Nichol, a Dutch girl, working at their embassy. She is outspoken, amusing and vivacious, full of good intentions and energy which fortunately she releases weekly on the rugby field, for which all are indeed truly grateful.

Dimi has now married a French lady, Marie, chic as only the French can be, but ambitious and already well-versed in the gemstone trade, which Dimi has now entered successfully.

However the trade is full of fraudsters, crooks and thieves and as he builds, so many wish him ill and try to undermine his perseverance. One small quantity of gemstones was about to be shipped by a reputable airline but went missing. The family was outraged.

'Who perpetrated this crime?' cried Stella furiously. 'Do you know?' she asked the boys.

'We are sure but not quite certain,' replied Dimi.

'Then go and shoot them!' she ordered.

Dimi soothed her. 'You can't behave like that nowadays,' he said.

Stella was not to be appeased, and became even more excitable, as did the parrot, and with considerable melodrama, lamented: 'You are my sons are you not? You are my own flesh and blood, my soul is alive within you, threaten, be vengeful and get those stones back!'

Dimi and I went to the airlines office and met a staff member. After a sharp discussion of little consequence we got up then, leaning over the desk, Dimi said quietly but with menace: 'Those stones are to be in my office at 9.00 a.m. tomorrow, wherever they may be, do you understand?'

A sudden hush descended, those in adjacent offices shuddered at the masked threat. Everybody knew. The final scene was now being acted, not to be trivialized; the air was still and cool. We left.

Indeed the stones were returned at 9.00 a.m. Everybody was pleased except Mama Stella who felt there had been insufficient drama to the proceedings, as did the parrot, whose vocabulary had widened considerably.

*****

Life has indeed changed. The shackles of socialism have been thrown off. The cry, so heartfelt ten years before, has been listened to and the government under President Mwinyi, the successor to President Nyerere, has started to open up the economy, thereby encouraging the spirit of free enterprise which all Tanzanians and expatriates longed for.

This opening up of the economy unfortunately has affected the Mantheakis butchery for their usual clientele now seek their meat from supermarkets which have begun to spring up around town.

Business has faltered on the farm and poor Minas finds solace in growing tomatoes, melons and vegetables, which he cultivates and tends with care, selling to hotels and restaurants. Until, as it so often happens, others undercut his market and he is left with vague promises of purchase from his clients rather than firm orders. His business declines, as is the norm in Africa, fruitfulness followed by drought.

Likewise Yanni is looking for inspiration; he has constructed a brick building machine. It works and is successful and could have revolutionized the building industry, but lack of capital and competition, which always seems to frustrate ambition, have become major constraints to his inventive nature.

*****

'And why are you here?' I am asked, as lifestyles and livelihoods became intertwined in the conversation.

'I am on my way to Indonesia,' I tell them.

'Quite a detour, not the most direct route,' suggests John quizzically.

'No, but I am going to Tanga first. Jane Tamé has problems, money as usual and has asked me if I would be interested in purchasing some

197

of Kwamtili Estate's shares.'

A frown fades over Stella's good humour.

'Anybody even thinking of ploughing money into a plantation must be mad, even those who know about them.' She looks at me severely. 'The easiest way to lose money is to invest in a sisal plantation.'

'Kwamtili is cocoa,' I reply doggedly.

'It's all the same,' she warns me, 'there is no future in the plantation industry.'

*****

Many of the older generation of plantation owners had bad reputations, particularly concerning gambling, followed closely by women. It was not uncommon for an estate to change ownership on the single throw of a dice, a busted flush or a wrong call at poker.

Wives also were on occasions dangled as a prize; for a player having lost his money was quite willing to gamble his wife away rather than lose his estate.

With these thoughts in mind I leave the farm, pick up a gas refrigerator that I had imported, and, with Minas hanging onto the fridge, we depart for Tanga thence to Kwamtili, eight hours away.

Debts to pay off, shopkeepers unpaid for months; banks crying out for their loans to be repaid, or, we will take the estate over, they threaten. Unlikely, I think, who in a bank could ever manage Kwamtili or even want to? Only a person with diminished responsibility would ever buy an estate like Kwamtili.

Driving to Kwamtili with the fridge and Minas

40

Kwamtili Estate

So it came to pass that after a prolonged drinking bout with Jane Tamé and friends, when sensibilities become fuzzy and warm and optimism overrides any misgivings and constraints, which under normal circumstances would have ordered, wait and reflect, I became the proud owner of Kwamtili Estate Ltd with 65% of the shares.

The estate was founded by a family firm from Hamburg in the days of Kaiser Wilhelm II and enjoyed a long life of unprofitability. Bananas first, because the Germans liked very much eating the fruit. When that crop failed, coffee was planted, which after a few good years succumbed to coffee berry disease and rust. Then more bananas, because the Germans still pined for there amatory flavour. But, similar to the original plantings, they soon succumbed to pestilence and the owners then planted oil palms which were unsuccessful because nobody knew how to cut the bunches off the palm, and, in desperation, instead cut the palms down in order to harvest the bunches ... and that was the end of the oil palm project.

The family from Hamburg gradually lost interest and departed, selling the property to Freddie Tamé who later married Jane, an ex BOAC airhostess, in 1961.

Freddie owned many sisal properties but owing to the low market price of sisal rope, due to the advent of synthetic fibres, plantations became economically unviable and many owners were made bankrupt, including Mr. Tamé. Jane, who had also trained as a bookkeeper, tried her best to keep the estates solvent. Unfortunately she failed and the only estate that remained in their possession was Kwamtili.

Even during the darkest periods of nationalisation in the late 1960s and 1970s, Jane kept hold of Kwamtili, and President Nyerere, who had begun to realise that nationalising the country's assets was not the best way forward, allowed Kwamtili to remain in her hands.

*****

Kwamtili is located in a picturesque valley of the Usambara Mountains 2½ hours from Tanga. How or why the Hamburg family had chosen this exact location is not fully understood for the soils are gravelly, rocky in parts and not particularly fertile. However it certainly is beautiful, with the house built cresting a small hill overlooking a swirling river in the valley below. Birds and butterflies of every description dance among the trees, a watchers' paradise. Probably the family was out to impress, for plantation owners had acquired the best land during those years when the kings of Tanzania were the sisal growers.

*****

Jane now lived in Tanga, at a prime location in the middle of town. Her house had been taken over by the government under the national housing scheme in the 1970s and it still had not been returned to her.

State ownership of everything had pervaded society during this period, a policy advised by uncouth, saturnine European and Russian advisors who courted the government as obsequious salesmen promote their wares.

The economic miracles, conjured up by the press worldwide, to promote socialism, were but a veneer, disguising the mediocrity and poverty of thought, mind and deed which then existed and upon which Tanzania and similar African, and some European, governments latched upon as a cure to their economic and social ills.

Meanwhile at Kwamtili Estate Ltd. the flow of investment had dried

202

up. In 1961, cocoa, specie Criollo, was planted. Annual production varied between 15 and 40 tonnes. Not very much, but the price of Criollo cocoa always earned a premium, being considered more desirable than the beans from hybrid varieties used in bulk cocoa processing.

Poor Jane was in the process of losing more or less everything. The estate was a burden, consuming considerable sums of borrowed money, with only bank loans keeping the company and herself alive.

*****

I did, of course, do all the things that Stella advised me not to. I invested heavily in the estate, paying off the debts. I put Jane in charge of the accounts but fortuitously recognised early on that, for Jane, any funds to the estate's credit may be used as she pleased, which was not always to the benefit of the estate. I had to admire her fortitude as the funds dried up, obliging her to present to all and sundry an image of self-sufficiency without the means to do so. She offered a pretence of poise and calmness as I took control of the estate's finances and Jane's income was brought in line with that of the other staff.

Equally debilitating was that the estate appeared to function as a paternalistic charity. Workers abounded, there were five clerical staff, two managers and a whole range of old retainers who were labelled as foremen, but would be found supervising only one worker daily.

I went about reducing overheads. Many of the old, the infirm and the sickly, for there were at least fifty workers and staff who were continually on some form of medication or on sick leave, were pensioned off. Malaria was rife and during my six years on Kwamtili, I caught malaria at least ten times, while for others the parasite had settled in their liver permanently, thereby seemingly impossible to eradicate.

*****

There was always confusion as to whether a person had malaria or

AIDS, or had succumbed to alcoholic poisoning, which was also prevalent. The symptoms for all appeared the same. Blood tests were taken but a positive result after an AIDs test appeared to be linked to the number of times the patient had had malaria.

For the first year I cut costs, overheads, staff, workers and, of course, Jane's reimbursement and the upkeep of the Tanga office.

New areas of cocoa were established and we started planting pepper vines, cashew and teak trees plus some exotica, for example, Straphanthos kombe, a vine which produces a stimulant for medical purposes. Being a natural product it possessed considerable marketing potential.

Everybody laboured hard to achieve success. Fortunately the price of cocoa rose and our harvests in 1994 and 1995 were most satisfactory. We contacted our usual buyers, a firm in Holland who, on receiving the samples, offered a price well below the world market price.

'Why,' I asked Jane, 'are we selling to these people? Each year they quote a miserly price and then make a huge profit.'

'Because,' she said, 'we always have sold to them. They have helped us out when we were short of cash in the past,' she answered.

'This is ridiculous! If they paid us the market price we would not be short of funds. They are holding us to ransom!' I replied.

I contacted buyers in London and then Switzerland and into our lives stepped Willy Mayer, entrepreneur, businessman and head of a Swiss charitable foundation which helped businesses and projects in the developing world.

He was knowledgeable and, after sending him a series of Criollo samples, he agreed to pay us £200 above the world market price. Our cocoa was much sought after, there being so little grown worldwide. The price was right.

Although Willy and I communicated frequently, I had purchased a satellite telephone by then, we did not become acquainted until 1996 when we met at the Royal Overseas League Club. Small of stature, he reminded me of M. Poirot of Agatha Christie fame. Willy never let us down.

'If you had fermented and dried your cocoa properly,' replied the Dutch in Amsterdam, grumpily, 'we would have given you the same price', when they learnt that they had lost the contract.

'Balls,' I replied, 'you have sucked Kwamtili dry for years.'

'But low prices have been endemic for the past five years,' they groaned. 'Yes, but during the mid 1980s when the cocoa price reached record levels, your payouts were equally derisory.'

And that was the end of our relationship with the Dutch in Amsterdam.

Market prices then declined and I had to inject funds to pay for salaries. As I was also working in Indonesia, (on a commodity crop project) this helped financially, while Julia divided her time between England, where she was teaching, and Indonesia where she also had a job teaching woodwind instrumentalists at the various academies and schools which abounded in Jakarta. Our lives seemed to slip effortlessly from continent to continent, although we didn't always meet up at the same place or at the same time.

On Kwamtili, Charles Cooke, formerly of the Mysore Lancers, ex-Malaysia and Eve his wife, helped to look after the estate during my absence, which was frequent. They loved the estate and walked tirelessly up and down the hills, supervising the estate workers and factory, making sure the estate ran well. It was such a relief for me to know that somebody like Charles was there helping the estate manager.

At the same time he was ably assisted by the estate mechanic, Ramathani, who could speak English but was regarded as a complete rogue, capable of dipping his fingers into any pie should an opportunity arise.

He was quite capable of stripping a Land Rover, even removing a gearbox and reassembling it. Not always as the manuals prescribed, but his confidence was so infectious that you allowed him to do whatever he thought necessary, whether it was repairing a drier, a tractor or the Land Rovers. Nothing was beyond him. He was impressive in his ability to overcome all problems and, even if he couldn't, never gave up.

Once, when Tanga was short of diesel and the price had risen to an exorbitant level, Ramathani left the estate with a troop of bicyclists plus jerry cans, climbed the mountains to reach Kenya and there filled up with diesel. It was cheaper than buying the fuel two hours away in Tanga.

*****

We all became cost conscious as the price of cocoa dipped further in 1997.

In order to increase our saleable volume we purchased from the local smallholders and also from the JKT (the National Service Unit) at Maramba, a market town not far away, where a Colonel Mapande was officer in charge.

I met him every Sunday, at what he referred to as the Maramba Club, a broken-down shack located on the main dust track which ran through the town centre, and which served as a hotel, bar and a den of iniquity and vice. Often we were joined there by the local police sergeant, who was continually sick with malaria, but which did not stop him drinking copious quantities of beer. The veterinary officer was a constant companion, likewise the odd sisal planter and farmer.

It was a very happy gathering and by late afternoon we broke ranks and I departed for Kwamtili with a Land Rover full of workers who had come to market to buy provisions. A long wheelbase Land Rover, to those readers untutored in such matters, can accommodate thirty-two fully grown Tanzanians, and that does not include those on the roof, although this was not generally allowed, as I was concerned that the roof would become dented.

Colonel Mapande, who I became very fond of, sadly died, probably drink hastened his demise, but his presence is still very much remembered in Maramba.

*****

In 1997 we enjoyed, as a family, Christmas on Kwamtili. It was also the first time that the children ate giraffe meat, which the army had shot to feed their conscripts.

At New Year, 1998, we joined up with the officers to celebrate. It was great fun, dancing, drinking and eating. Giraffe meat was on the menu. The soldiers loved it, Julia and I were brave, while the children brought up to eat everything on their plates nibbled tentatively wishing they had a school meal in front of them instead of a slice of haunch. It was tasty and lean, had it been fatty probably we would have surrendered as a family unit.

*****

Malaria was endemic throughout Tanga region and particularly severe in Maramba and Kwamtili, I caught it and treated myself with Halfan, a drug permitted in Tanzania although not allowed in the UK, but very effective.

Rachel was the only member of the family who never caught malaria. Frank, like me, was prone to the parasite and was on two occasions hospitalised on his return to school after a holiday on the Estate.

On one occasion, Rebecca, who was in her teens, 16 years old, wishing to participate in the nightlife of Tanga, drove to town with Hashim, the cook, in attendance.

Realising that she had malaria she sought out a doctor who gave her quinine tablets to take. Feeling unwell she returned with Hashim almost delirious, drove over a rock denting the front differential which then sprang a hairline leak.

However she drove on, arrived at the estate and collapsed. Meanwhile Ramathani, who was mooching around the neighbouring village of Muheza after work, seeing a thin line of dripping oil decided to follow it, conjuring up in his mind a vehicle in distress, which meant business and money, not realising that it was mine. He followed the

207

trail like a bloodhound; into the estate where the main access track passed through and then further on, to the villages beyond.

On meeting some passing workers he was told the vehicle was mine, whereupon he hurried up to the house to find out what had happened and to help, as he always did.

41

The Last of the Veterans

Whenever I had some free time in Indonesia I caught a flight from Jakarta to Dubai and then on to Dar es Salaam or Nairobi, for the connections were good. I would then stay a few days on the Estate and return to Jakarta.

It was tiring but fun. At each visit Jane looked a little older but still she retained her gracious caring demeanour, even when money was in short supply. She seldom went to the estate but busied herself with charity work, the Rotary, the hospital and the German war graves. For Freddie Tamé, now deceased, was part-German, part-Syrian and his loyalty lay more with the Germans than the British.

Because of this connection Jane was asked by the German Embassy if she would preside over the War Veteran's Committee, and each year she handed over what was called the Kaisers shilling to veterans who had served with General Von Lettow Vorbeck's German forces during World War I. She, needless to say, performed this duty with aplomb and dignity.

However as time went on, she noticed that, inexplicably, the number of veterans was increasing instead of declining, as is the usual case when old people grow even older.

Her worries were compounded by suddenly finding forty-year-olds requesting the shilling and even a twenty-year-old boy.

To ascertain who was genuine and who was not, she called the sergeant, a very old fellow, to shout out parade ground commands in

German and not in Swahili. Needless to say there was a lot of confusion, stumbling about and falling around by those who knew no German. The ranks of the receivers were in consequence thinned dramatically.

The next year there were still too many young veterans, who by now had learned the German commands. Jane's only recourse was to halve the amount of shillings per soldier. Which infuriated those who were genuine soldiers, who then turned upon the imposters, kicking them off the parade ground.

Thus dignity and discipline and pride were restored to these old men of the German fighting forces.

*****

Frank came out one holiday and we started expanding our new venture, a teak plantation. We purchased seedlings from the local forestry officer, Mr. Mkange, who would saunter up to the house most evenings to have a beer and regale me with his latest medical misfortunes.

I liked him immensely but could not take his supposed illnesses and malignancies too seriously. He also found Hashim's wife temptingly attractive and yearned for her daily, or whenever I met up with him, which was frequent.

During our evening sojourns we would often listen to the villagers drumming; rhythmically, precise, played with deft skills which seductively echoed up from the valley below. Sometimes we slithered down the hill from the house, waded the river and joined in the dancing and merriment on the other side. These were magical evenings which continued until early morning, when cockerels in the villages signalled that time was up.

I should have been more thoughtful and kind to Mr. Mkange, for arriving at the house one evening breathing heavily, he complained of

210

chest pains. 'You always have chest pains.' I told him, 'I am sure you are as fit as a fiddle. A beer will cure all your complaints.' He was sadly not as fit as a fiddle. One day he went to Tanga to have a medical check-up and did not return; he died of a heart attack.

I was really sad for he was a companionable, knowledgeable person. He knew the forest trees and took great pleasure in the magnificence of the mountainous jungle terrain in which he roamed, and at the same time he enjoyed the convivial evenings of friendship at Kwamtili.

*****

Our teak plantation grew in size. Frank helped by driving the Land Rover full of seedlings from the nursery to the field a few miles away. He enjoyed a firm friendship with Dustan, whose career on Kwamtili was difficult to decipher. Sometime askari (watchman), lining fundi (the person who lines up for planting), sometime hunter, guide, office boy, water carrier. He was immensely useful and reliable except when under the influence of drink.

On many occasions I tripped over his inert prone body lying outside across the house's front door, spear by his side, clutching a bow and arrow. Always sound asleep, but he worked all hours, though I was never quite sure on a daily basis, at what.

It was Dustan who arrived at my house one early morning with Joyce, the office typist/clerk and assistant dresser. They both looked worried, but not scared, as though some mild misfortune had befallen them and which some payment would be needed to cure. Money, or lack of it, was always at the hub of solving most mishaps.

'What's wrong?' I asked, as they stood on the veranda.

'My son has run away into the mountains,' said Joyce.

'Why?' I asked.

'He has done a very bad thing,' she answered.

211

Her son was a lively boy but well brought up, as were all Joyce's children.

'He killed your gardener last night,' she said.

'That's a pity,' I answered curtly, 'he was a very good gardener. Isn't he your eldest son?' I asked Dustan.

The reply came back in the affirmative.

'You will have to go and report to the police at Maramba,' I told them.

They realised that it was their duty to do so.

'I need Tshs 10,000 ($7.00), for the police,' she said.

'And what about Dustan?' I queried. 'He has lost his son.'

There was quiet. 'I need an advance to pay him too,' said Joyce, 'but not very much, because it was his son, according to witnesses, who started the trouble.'

Dustan agreed that this was indeed the case. So honest and honourable in such dealings.

'Where is the dead boy?' I asked.

'Under a cashew nut tree down by the path, at the bottom of your garden, the big one full of nuts. He is not in a nice condition, all little bits.'

Probably not, I thought.

'You had better gather him up and bury him at the church on the hill,' and went inside to fetch some money.

The boy was buried. Joyce's son did not return for he ran away into the mountains, and Dustan had lost his eldest in a senseless fight caused by the smoking of bangi, a drug made out of hemp. It was always the same on Kwamtili; drugs induced violence. Pombe (an alcoholic drink) just sent everybody to sleep or to have sex, never to crime.

*****

Such an episode of drug-induced murder was fortunately rare in the villages. However underneath the rural dwellers' quiet and forgiving demeanour lurked a tide of frustration and despair fuelled by the daily drudgery they had to endure. And at the same time penury and continual surges of debilitating pestilence plagued and fatigued them to a state of rural bondage.

From the countryside the young fled to the towns to seek a better life, a pot of gold, a sustainable lifestyle. But sadly not for long, as there was little employment and endemic roguery which pervaded throughout urban society forced them into a life of chance and later disillusionment.

Meanwhile during this period, the late 1990s, I had purchased a plot of land close to Mbutu Gomvu, a village 30 miles south of Dar es Salaam, overlooking an exquisite beach inhabited by turtles, a few local fishermen and an occasional sauntering lion and there, on a small plateau of rocky coral, we started to build a home which would cement our affiliation to this turbulent but beautiful African shore.

42

Subsistence Farming in Indonesia

A reader might suppose that for a lot of the time I was very much involved at Kwamtili Estate rather than fulfilling my duties in Indonesia as Agronomist with the Smallholder Commodity Crop Project (SCCP) funded by the World Bank. They of course would be quite wrong, for my brief visits to Tanzania were undertaken during my days off, public holidays, of which there were many, and longish weekends. A lot of night-time travelling but worth the effort.

SCCP fully consumed me, for it involved thousands of smallholders and approximately 370,000 hectares of rubber and coconuts. It necessitated journeying the full distance of this thousand island archipelago, from top to bottom, north Sumatra to the Moluccas. Flying from Jakarta to Ambon, the capital of the Moluccas Islands, could take a full day depending on connections.

*****

The project was effective in that it provided commodity crop involvement for settled smallholders, not transmigrants, who benefited from the sale of their products. A welcome addition to their household incomes.

Most of the farmers were diligent and keen, the Javanese in particular were generally excellent farmers. I was full of admiration of their endeavours.

They were especially brilliant paddy (rice) farmers, able to irrigate their fields with precision, ensuring the correct shape, size and depth of the channels, whether the area planted happened to be valley slopes or bottoms. Their talent, in my experience, almost unique, although the Balinese also were skilful paddy farmers.

In Malaysia we all used Javanese labourers to de-silt the estate's drains, large or small, and before mechanical equipment became more widely employed, Javanese were recruited to open up drainage networks, whatever the configuration and over any terrain.

Wherever one travelled in this straggling archipelago of islands, Javanese farmers could be found trying to make a living, seeking to build a new life and many also had joined the transmigration schemes, for Java was densely populated and its land over-exploited. Although the desire to migrate was never strong, it was regarded as a necessity; Java could not sustain the ever growing population seeking sustenance from the exhausted soils of their homeland.

*****

The project tried to cater for the many thousands of farmers eking out a living from the land. Areas in need of assistance had been earmarked a decade earlier and the scheme was well underway at the time of my arrival on the scene.

It was working well, farmer households were benefiting from the sale of their rubber or copra. Incomes improved as the rubber and coconut plantings matured, and businessmen soon realized the commercial potential on offer as product volumes increased.

Although only one hectare of planting material was offered to each farmer by the project, plus inputs, all to be repaid, many farmers, realising the benefits, expanded their commodity crop area. This resulted in the development of smallholder estates, managed by the individual farmers residing there.

*****

On the Moluccas, which I visited periodically, the project, although well received, lacked impetus. Government agency assistance was desultory and being far away from Jakarta resulted in fitful commitment.

There were also many environmental problems. Drought, insect damage, frequent wild pig incursion, lack of fertilizer, all the village males fishing or logging, all the females breeding.

To reach the project area on Ceram Island, and its regional capital Amahai, you had to journey by ferry to Pira and then by coastal road.

It was a pretty drive; past small groves of cloves and a wide range of fruit trees, the durian especially prominent. Over fast flowing rivers, through forest and along the sea shore. Past villages of limestone white houses, where mosques and churches had been built to neighbour each other, not to compete for clientele but as a status of togetherness and the celebration of one Deity.

A happy state of affairs for all to perceive and rejoice in but which sadly disintegrated throughout the Moluccas during those months of madness in 1999 and 2000 when Muslims and Christians destroyed the harmony of their relationship by murder and mayhem, all in the name of Mohammed and Jesus, unable to converge, to remain disparate in word and deed and thereby ultimately resulting in strife.

*****

After two hours of driving we arrived at our project sites, where poor villagers lived off sago flour, rice and cassava; earning incomes marginal even for subsistence. I enjoyed my visits but despaired at the lack of progress. Except for fishing there was very little to sustain the communities, many of the young sought work in Amahai or in Ambon. A cocoa plantation had been established by PTP IV, and the World Bank had earmarked funds for other ventures.

Plans to introduce hybrid rice and maize into the region had failed miserably. Demonstration blocks were established by the Government and a major seed company heralded the advantages of hybrid seed, which would help alleviate malnutrition.

The rice was planted and grew. Then the fertilizer was late arriving and then the rains failed and then the irrigation system silted up and then, inevitably, the insects invaded.

We watched, dismayed. What hope for the villagers if these sponsored demonstration plots could not be implemented satisfactorily in order to show how these so called wonder strains could be promoted for farmer usage?

However, fortunately the farmers, while tentatively watching and observing the trials, continued to plant their own selections of seed. Seed which had been passed down from generation to generation; seed cherished, selected for adaptability and yield, which, although less than normal, was sustainable year in, year out. And, even able to withstand the scorching dry winds which annually savaged the land and fanned the polluting fires, destroying large tracts of forest as farmers slashed and tilled, searching for a fertile top soil in which to grow their crops.

Meanwhile the timber barons, hungry for profit, continued to harvest the hardwoods; scouring the landscape with their bulldozers, denuding it of any remaining precious vegetation, redefining in the process, and to its detriment, the existing soil profile and the water catchment basin which could affect a whole region's drainage system.

Indeed the seed needed to be very robust, hybrids were not the answer.

Ceram Sea

Buru

Piru
Ceram
Amahai
Ambon

MALUKU   Banda

Banda Sea

South Banda Basin

Dili
E. Timor

Timor Sea

W. Timor
Kupang

Towns : Piru   Dili
         Amahai   Kupang
         Ambon

Australia

219

43

Pollution Over Ambon

The drought of 1998 was one of the worst to afflict Indonesia. Forest fires swept the landscape, smoke and debris blew across the Malacca straits to Singapore and Kuala Lumpur. Masks covering faces became grimed with ash from the burning forests.

Cries of outrage worldwide accompanied the billowing black clouds which streamed northwards with the prevailing winds.

I was in Ambon when the airlines called a halt to any further air travel. The airport was closed. The passengers listless, waiting, lay in nooks and crannies and on the floor hoping for the smog to clear.

At the hotels waiting passengers tried to get news. There was none. I drove to the airport and climbed up the stairs to the control tower.

'Salamat pagi,' (good morning) I called jovially, 'any news of arrivals or departures?'

The air controllers, having nothing better to do, were playing cards.

'No,' they chorused, 'this dense smoggy cloud is not going to go away quickly.'

'What height is the cloud?' I asked.

'2000 - 3000 ft and drifting upward,' came back the reply.

'Well that shouldn't be a problem for your new beautiful modern aircraft,' I said.

'It isn't,' they replied, 'but if anything happened and they had to return visibility over the airport is below the limit.'

'Look,' I said, 'I can see the other side of the runaway, take off and within a few minutes you are out of the gloom and into bright, beautifully blissful clear sky up above. It's a doddle!' I cried.

'Can't lah,' they replied, 'not allowed. Why don't you ask the mission pilots to fly you out? They are going to Kupang on Timor Island (the Flores) and could give you a lift.'

'Well if you allow them to take off, why not a commercial plane?'

Smiles all round.

'Because,' one of the controllers said, 'the pilots don't want to, two are of pensionable age, the younger ones probably have got girlfriends, therefore they are quite happy to lounge about at their hotel. And,' chuckles all around, 'the mission plane is at Amahai, on a small strip which we, in the tower, have no jurisdiction over. So they can take off whenever they like, but if they get lost and crash it will certainly cost them and their lives too, probably.'

I galloped off to the mission.

44

Evacuation by Mission Air

I had tremendous respect for the Benedictine Brothers in Tanzania who farmed the lands around their monasteries, provided vocational training to the young, administered to the sick and brought business professionalism to the communities. Even the nuns attached to the Brothers' holy orders' were hard working and committed.

Unfortunately, in contrast, other missions, such as the Anglicans, appeared to care only about saving the souls of their followers and seldom did much for the communities in which they resided. Probably breaking bread at communion being the most onerous activity they had to undertake in their various parishes.

*****

The mission, with the plane, was not far from the airport and belonged to one of the breakaway evangelical units of the Anglican Church. The missionaries were mainly American, right wing and robust, brawny and unsympathetic to the meek and lowly.

'I understand you may be flying to Kupang sometime?' I asked a missionary standing under the shade of a mango tree, ruminating, probably, about the weather or who to discipline next.

'Why do you want to know?' he asked me uncivilly.

'Because I would happily pay for a lift out.'

He looked at me, a mask over his ruddy face. 'It will cost you,' he said.

'How much?' I asked.

'US$500,' he answered, a grim smirk on his face.

'This man is behaving in a most ungodly fashion', I thought to myself.

'I could fly Concorde to Kupang for $500,' I said.

'Can you pilot a plane?' he asked, to which I answered in the affirmative. 'Can you get another four passengers? Then the price will only be US$100 each.' I agreed.

'And, if I persuade another four to join us when do we depart?' I asked.

'On Friday,' he answered, 'I have a service to conduct on Saturday.'

'Oh, so you are going there anyway!' I interrupted.

'Yes, and now that the good Lord has delivered you to me I can fly free of charge to Kupang and use the money to serve the Lord.'

'Booze,' I thought, for I could smell his breath.

It all sounded like profiteering to me, surely there is something in the Bible about helping those in distress and providing succour to those in need? Oh well, back to town.

I drove to my hotel to seek others willing to pay to fly to Kupang.

I hunted high and low but nobody was interested. 'Too dangerous ... a small plane ... in this smog ... saya takut' (I am scared). I left the hotel and walked down to the docks.

On the way I stopped at a coffee shop, there was a small gaggle of foreigners sipping coffee. I went in and sat down. I listened to their talk. They wanted to get out, they were a film crew.

'I have a plane and four seats if you want,' I said loudly in their direction, joining the conversation. They turned around.

'You have? Really?' exclaimed one.

'Yes US$100 per person.'

There was excited discussion then a pretty girl got up and walked over.

'My name is Genevieve Taylor,' she said, 'do you honestly have room? We have been making a documentary film on Banda Island and must return to Jakarta as soon as possible.'

*****

I explained the situation.

'We have to go to Amahai and then the mission pilot will take us to Kupang in Timor and from there we can get a commercial flight to Jakarta.'

It was agreed that three of them would come, Genevieve and the cameramen Roger and Pete. This meant I had to find one other and back again to the hotel I walked. I couldn't believe there was nobody willing to pay $100 to depart Ambon.

I told the reception clerk to start looking. In the hotel there was the usual hustle and bustle, all enquiring, hoping for better news. I went to my room.

No sooner was I inside when the telephone rang and a voice enquired about a seat.

'Yes, I have one left,' I told the voice. 'Who are you?' I asked.

He was Japanese and came frequently to Ambon to buy pearls from the rich beds which had been laid down off the coast.

I breathed a sigh of relief and told him to stand by at the Amahai airfield tomorrow morning. He confirmed he would be there.

*****

Next morning everybody was present and ready to leave. The missionary was already inspecting the plane and the fuel tanks were being filled up.

We handed over the money, which he accepted ungraciously without a word, and we climbed into the plane. I sat in the front.

225

The pollution was not as chronic here as across the waters at Ambon, but still the sky was grey and a thick mist of fluttering debris began to surge over the airfield. This gradually thickened as the early morning breezes, after a calm night, agitated the smouldering fires in the hills surrounding the town.

The missionary did his checks and with open palms prayed to the Lord for a safe journey. 'Amen,' we all said.

We took off into the gathering gloom. The airspace seemed to be clogged with smoke and forest wreckage; upward we struggled, bumping against the rushing smoke. All quiet in the plane.

Radio static suddenly alerted us.

'It's Ambon control,' I told him, 'you had better answer or they will send out a search party and that will cost you,' I said with sour good humour.

He looked at me grimly. 'I will take over,' I said, 'then you can keep in touch and navigate.'

He nodded, and I took control.

The plane burped and slurped through the sky, its propellers coughing out the filthy air, longing to be free, and then, suddenly, we were through, we had escaped, and the plane seemed to take on a new lease of life as we climbed into an unlimited horizon of deep blue sky, 8,000 ft up.

We all breathed a sigh of relief. 'Kupang here we come,' I thought. At least there should be no pollution in Timor.

*****

I gave Genevieve, Roger and Pete a lift into Jakarta once we had arrived back. Her documentary on the nutmeg industry of Banda Island, an island some distance south east of the Moluccas, was a success, although unfortunately I never saw the film.

Flying through the smog from Ceram

45

Presidential Elections

In Jakarta Julia and I had rented a small apartment above an antique shop on Jalan (road) Semerang in Menteng district, a most desirable location, close to the city centre and not far from one of President Suhartos' town residences.

It could be described by property agencies as being upmarket. Some might disagree and would say not so upmarket, for presidential elections were about to be held and wandering tribes of rival supporters snarled the streets.

We loved the apartment, for it was clothed with a magnificent collection of pictures, principally Balinese village scenes and ceremonies of a religious nature, exquisitely painted, expensively valued; fortunately not for sale and hung in our rooms because the owner had run out of wall space on which to spread her collection.

The shop, or boutique, as it was called, belonged to Emelie Gandanegara, an old left-over Dutch lady, previously married to an Indonesian, who also owned a small hotel complex on Bali Island and the poshest restaurant in town, which probably served the finest Indonesian cuisine anywhere in the world.

She was forthright in her views and excellent company, spoke perfect English and was a third generation Dutch Indonesian.

Owning a property in Bali meant that she could divide her time between the island and Jakarta, always making her escape from the city when the weather either turned too hot or too wet, or when social unrest was about to flare-up amongst Jakarta's poor and restless citizens, which happened sporadically throughout the year.

Then off she would trot, with an entourage of five and two vehicles. She disliked flying and would instead travel the length of Java to Surabaya, stopping off and visiting the remnants of old Dutch society who could be found sprinkled amongst the estates and hills of Java.

In Bali she would remain until the heat, flooding, water shortages or unrest had subsided in Jakarta, and then she would return the same way as she had come.

*****

When not outstation I commuted to the Ministry of Agriculture, where the project had a floor to itself.

Early morning, before Julia had awoken, I walked to an adjacent park next to the mayor's house.   There I would thumb down a taxi in order to drive to our offices, located next to the zoo at Sennayan.

Our staff numbered seventy-three. By the time I arrived they had already plugged into their computers, or were entering up their ledgers; finalizing plans, or trying to make the best deals regarding the purchase of fertilizers and other materials.

Next door was the senior Indonesian's project office, close by to the consultants' offices, easy to call those in residence, although always one or two of us were away.

We were a mixed bag; an American, John Fenton with old world charm and manners. He had worked in Iran and was an IT expert. There were two Filipinos; one attached to the extension services and the other to finance. Dominique Boutaine, a French agronomist, diligent and knowledgeable, was usually to be found on the island of Suluwezi at his coconut nurseries.

After work, which may have included, other than my normal duties, writing a speech for the Director General of Estates, briefing a Minister on a subject which he was to discourse upon, anything from seed viability to water well depth in Lampung, South Sumatra, I would grab a taxi and return to Menteng. There, to await Julia's return from downtown Jakarta where she was teaching a rich mix of children at the International School. Crowded streets, jammed traffic, exuberant supporters of both electoral parties, often impeded her progress and she always arrived late and tired.

Reverberations of discontent, mid 1998, increased daily as the elections drew near. The opposition party's offices were close to Jalan Semerang, located under the railway viaduct, and were continually harassed by the police and army. However, as Megawati Soekarno, the daughter of the first President, Bapak Soekarno, a charismatic leader, often referred to as the father of the nation, was now the figurehead leader of the socialist party, the police could do little to thwart the ambitions of her members. Especially as modern communications could transmit at the press of a button any skulduggery; in an instant the world would know.

As the election drew closer, and swathes of supporters on both sides of the political spectrum crowded the city's highways and alleys, Emelie decided to retreat to her Bali refuge.

Regally bestowing gifts upon her staff and telling them to behave and work hard, Emilie, cushioned between her faithful entourage, drove slowly out of Jakarta and southwards.

Her sudden departure influenced Julia, who decided Bali and Emilie's garden boutique hotel would be a preferable option during these troubled days. Daily interference by a mass of screeching undesirables as she journeyed to and from the schools and music conservatories was getting on her nerves.

Enough, she said, arriving back in a battered taxi one evening, the driver looking fraught and shaken, keeping himself awake by smoking endless clove-filled cigarettes. For, as the election campaign began edging toward a climax, so supporters of both parties multiplied on the streets. They banged on car windows, red-eyed, almost amok, mouthing expletives at the hapless passengers inside the vehicles. A car journey had indeed become a very unpleasant experience.

'I am going to Bail,' she said. 'With my luck if I remain here, I will get trapped in a fight and that will be the end of little me.'

What would granny say if Julia was mugged or hijacked, I wondered. The British navy was no longer committed to rescuing stranded taxpayers in an emergency.

'You must leave at once,' I commanded, 'I will buy you a ticket.'

*****

Meanwhile, unbeknown to us, Rebecca had also decided to visit Jakarta, although we thought she was safe in Spain with a school friend.

While Julia was happily ensconced in Bali, I received a phone call from a secretary, advising me a planter friend of mine, Pat Basket, was in town, would I meet him at the Hotel Indonesia. Of course I would, I replied.

Arriving at the hotel I looked around, hoping to see the tall, languid figure of Pat. No Pat, I went to the bar. Although now a Muslim and a reluctant teetotaller, having married Sue, a pretty Malay girl from Banting District, Selangor, I still had expected to find him commiserating with an orange juice while listening to the band. He wasn't.

I returned to the huge towering foyer of the hotel with its ornate decorated pillars, pictures of Bapak Soekarno meeting Robert Kennedy of the USA three decades previously, adorned the far wall.

I had first stayed at the hotel in 1966 just after the end of confrontation. It was then empty, a landmark, and except for the district of Menteng along one side, only fields of rice and the occasional kerbau (water buffalo) grazing contentedly in the distance could be observed from one's hotel bedroom window. Neither office block nor hotel littered the landscape; Jakarta now, forty years later, is a major city of at least sixteen million people.

It was while back-tracking to the reception that a figure darted out from behind a pillar and placed two hands over my eyes.

'Guess who?' a voice asked.

'What are you doing here?' I answered, 'I thought you were in Spain', as Rebecca removed her hands.

'I decided to come to Jakarta instead.'

'Are you the friend I am supposed to meet?' she confirmed she was. 'What are you doing here?' I asked.

'I caught the wrong flight,' she answered.

I made no further enquiries.

'Where is mum?' she asked,

'Oh she has gone to Bali to avoid the electioneering and mobs. Better there than here,' I answered.

'Good, I will go there the day after tomorrow, that's if you buy me a ticket,' she said, 'I spent my last penny on a taxi from the airport.'

I was pleased, she was here, but a young girl taking a taxi ride from the airport was just not sensible. Jakarta was experiencing troubled times. It was not safe.

She stayed at the apartment and I arranged an office vehicle to take her to the airport.

'Have you seen Frank and Rachel?' I asked. 'Are they coming out after school?'

'No idea,' she replied, 'they had better not, with their fair skins and blonde hair they will probably get sold into slavery. It's a new up and coming industry, you know,' she continued. 'Oh well, being in a harem of a rich Arab potentate might be fun. Good food, I understand, and all the luxuries on tap.'

*****

Our offices did not close, but owing to transport problems and as vociferous hostilities between the parties heightened, less of the staff were able to travel to work, until on one day only eleven had arrived, plus John F. and myself.

To make matters worse, night curfews also hindered further movement and I was no longer able to walk to my favourite Makan Padang eating shops, even those located close by.

Thus there was little point in me staying any longer in Jakarta, so I packed my bag and left for Bali. John Fenton by now was happily ensconced behind the walls of the American club, secure from the bitterness outside.

Mr. Suharta lost, which resulted in turmoil and road blocks, manned by unsmiling, heavily armed soldiers. Probably many, particularly the middle classes, wished that he had been returned to power for when a strong man is defeated, the natives become restless and the resultant chaos, the usual legacy at the end of a forceful government, soon takes hold, much to the detriment of society.

46

A World Bank Mission

As calm returned, a World Bank (WB) team arrived in order to visit their projects.

The WB's representative was a very pleasant Bangladeshi with a forgettable name, so I called him Fred, being simple to remember. He did not seem to mind. He wrote concise erudite reports with all the salient points included.

Unlike other officers he was responsive and interested in smallholder subsistence farming, probably because he came from a poverty stricken country himself.

He knew little about agriculture but listened attentively, which was unusual for a consultant from the subcontinent of India and environs.

Fred visited all the project sites and, as funding for the two year contractual period was drawing to a close, a 'wrap-up' meeting was to be held In Jakarta, with a request for further funding included on the agenda. We were in no doubt that the Bank would be cajoled into providing for a project extension. As always the spectre of communism or the election of an unfriendly government would persuade them to issue another batch of dollars in order to preserve peace and social harmony.

*****

There were four officials from the Bank present at the so-called 'wrap-up' meeting, which I was asked to chair.

All the project consultants and their counterparts were present and procedures went well, without too much intellectual interference from the World Bank, none of whom knew anything about coconuts or rubber. All were economists, a narrow-minded breed, sums and cash flows, all decisions computer-derived and driven.

For them, although the project was about farmers, who they were or what they did or how they survived, was immaterial. Provided the budget had not been overspent and crookery was kept at an acceptable level, they were quite happy.

After a couple of hours, I thought we would be able to finish by early afternoon and so did the Bank officials, with only the renewal issue to be discussed. The meeting had, up to then, been amiable and reasonable.

'Are we finished?' I asked.

By early evening the demands made by the Indonesians had still not been settled; I was startled at their audacity and rudeness, not taking no for an answer. In contrast the Bank officials appeared supine and nervous in their deliberations.

At a tea break I suggested they rebut the Indonesians' demands. I felt really annoyed, as did the other project consultants. We want the money to continue, but implementation should be on our terms not the Indonesians, for they are the client with the begging bowl. Their attitude was unacceptable, particularly as a significant proportion of the funds would be siphoned off to various personages, all well-known and, without exception, for such skulduggery was becoming an issue worldwide.

*****

Of course the Indonesians got what they wanted, but we, the project consultants, also managed to ensure that the direction of the funding was our responsibility. More chest-beating by the Indonesians, but they were generally happy with the way the negotiations had resulted in more funds and another extension, which was pleasing for all concerned.

However once the meeting was over and the mission's personnel had said their farewells, we, the project consultants, arranged to meet them at their swish five star hotel later that evening.

'A celebration!' they chorused.

'Good, let's make the most of it,' we said to ourselves, 'they will pay.'

It was a pleasant evening until we pointed out that when a mission such as theirs so easily succumbed to berating Indonesian officialdom, the legacy, for all to see, was that by employing bullying tactics anything was possible, which in effect affected us, the project consultants, who were basically the implementors of the programmes.

'You should realize,' we told them, 'that you were negotiating from a position of strength, you hold the purse strings, not them, they are the supplicants, not you. It gives a bad impression. They thrive on arrogant displays of dominance, it's in their culture.'

Our convivial evening became no longer convivial. They did not like the way the conversation had sliced through their dignity. Their pride had been dented, but they also realised that politics, without regard to needs, now governed the funding process, leaving them powerless in the process.

*****

My two year contract came to an end, and I wanted to return to Kwamtili Estate. The Indonesians could not understand why I wanted to leave, in fact why would anybody want to leave such a successful project?

'Renew your contract,' they urged.

However I wanted to manage my own estate, Julia was quite happy to depart. The elections had given her a not altogether happy vision of Indonesia once the strong arm of Suharto had been rendered asunder.

237

47

Back to Africa

Nichol indeed was very lucky; she had seemingly charmed Michel into agreeing to marry her. Rebecca was quite put out for she had had designs on him since the age of six.

We all went to the wedding ceremony, held in the charming little Greek chapel on the farm at Kunduchi.

The evening's entertainment had been organised by the brothers and Scottie Coles, Michel's hunting partner at Miombo Safaris who, as compere and host, reigned supreme. Smart gents and stunning ladies abounded, Josette, Scottie's wife, exuded voluptuousness. Louanna, Anna, Marie, Julia, a multitude of Greek friends and relations provided a myriad of colour and beauty. Stella, so composed, glided across the stage, the perfect hostess; radiant and lovely.

However there was another wedding due. Louanna, the only daughter in the Mantheakis family, was to marry Gilberto, her American husband from a civil wedding and now both eager to consummate their marriage in a church on Sifnos, a Greek island. The year was 1999 one year after Nichol and Michel's marriage.

*****

Giberto was a pleasant American, good fun with a quick wit. However he was the despair of Stella, who appreciated the finer things in life and that included etiquette and manners. Once marriage was rumoured, Stella set about educating Gilberto in the simple delicacies of life that one should expect from a son-in-law.

Stilton cheese should be cut in such a manner that all the creamy end portions were not harvested at one go. Knives and forks were appropriate tools to use when eating, coffee was sipped not slurped and baseball hats should be worn outside the home and not inside at the dinner table.

As this was very much a long term project to be pursued at all costs by Stella, whenever we visited Kunduchi we were all riveted to see what progress had been made. We eagerly held our breath hoping to glimpse a breach of protocol during dinner.

Fortunately we were never disappointed and simultaneously with Stella we exaggerated our grimaces of disapproval, much to the amusement of all at the table, including Gilberto, who always played to the gallery and particularly Rachel who, if she should be present, blushed pink at every failure.

Even the parrot joined in and at the appropriate moment would release an audible sigh of disapproval as she strutted her perch murmuring to herself, head wagging in disapproval and, should ever a knife approach Gilberto's mouth instead of a fork, a squawk of indignation would echo around the veranda, followed by, 'Gilberto, Gilberto, Gilberto, no, no, no!'

Louanna and Gilberto were married; Julia and Rebecca attended the ceremony in Greece. I stayed at Kunduchi and celebrated the tying of their nuptial bonds with a stranger from Australia who was visiting Tanzania in order to promote the tea tree, which exuded an oil used in aromatherapy and contained a multitude of beneficial properties.

Other friends were also present and by midnight we had almost finished Nichol's supply of wine. Phone calls were received from Greece telling us that all was well and that Rebecca was now dancing topless on a table, later to be joined by Julia.

All were happy and content.

I eventually went to bed, for another day in Africa had started. Tomorrow I would return to our new house at Mbutu Gomvu, and then later, northward to Tanga and Kwamtili Estate. Not for long though, as Pat Basket, Principal Director of SOCFIN Estates Indonesia phoned and asked if I would like to join him and help manage their plantations. I accepted my career had turned full circle.

48

Bottoms Up

I arrived in Medan, Indonesia in 1999 and was surprised how quickly I adapted again to plantation life. Julia also was pleased to return.

Socfin, a Belgian company, was managed by my good friend, Pat Basket. Similar to most plantations it ran like clockwork. The production line of palm oil products and rubber was cost effective and efficiently produced.

There were very few foreign plantation companies left now, most were locally owned. Fortunately, however the high standards bequeathed from the past were still very much in evidence and the companies functioned just as competently as before.

Pat Basket was an anachronism, the very last of the planters left in the ring, he will never leave, he has me in tow now.

*****

Meanwhile, outside the industrial heartland of company estates, the tropical world of agriculture continued to evolve.

Agronomists had become a redundant species, having been replaced by economists and management experts who had taken over the reins of providing assistance to the rural poor. Government authorities were to be the providers of aid and patronage using funds issued by the first world. How governments loved this approach! Money for jam, and the first world just did not appear to understand that very little would ever reach the farmers.

Just as ADAB economists in the Philippines abhorred our direct response approach to the farmers, so 'bottoms up' became the catch phrase; help from below and build up the institutions to assist and supply what the farmers needed.

Unfortunately few farmers knew what they wanted. How do you know what you need if you have not been exposed to what might be possible? Money was to be made available in credit and loans.

'Good,' said the authorities, 'we will issue credit and loans, provided by the rich nations, for the benefit of the poor suffering farmers.'

'Better to scatter money from a plane flying above rather than giving it to the government,' was the usual terse response.

For a Tanzanian to repay a loan is very unusual, it is not part of his culture. Share, yes, but to repay money to a government authority is not an option which is taken seriously. On one of my infrequent visits to Kwamtili, an old Tanzanian farmer friend urged me to seek a loan to start a cashew nut enterprise.

'The loan is available,' he told me, 'hurry take it up.'

'If I take up a loan I have to repay it,' I told him. 'Which I can ill-afford.' 'What? Repay a loan?' he mused. 'Whatever for?'

'It is the rules,' I said, 'that's what a loan means.'

'If it is a grant,' he asks, 'do you have to repay it?'

'No, for a grant no repayment is necessary.'

'Good then I will call it a grant not a loan.'

He seemed satisfied with this interpretation and off he sped to Dar es Salaam, later to return with his 'grant'.

*****

Of course his cashew nut plantings flourished. But later, as the trees bore nuts, so did requests from the authorities seeking repayment of the loan start arriving. Neither the demand notes nor the arrival of sharp-suited bank officials looking for money dented his happy demeanour, for he had no intention of repaying the loan or 'grant', as he respectfully called it. And, all those in authority also knew he wouldn't.

His age held sway. Tanzanians respect old age and the bank's demands, although vigorous, lacked threat and within himself he just did not seem to care what action they might pursue.

I was pleased I had not entangled myself with a loan, for although sixty years of age, I knew that if I had, black suited bank officials would soon be trudging up to Kwamtili looking for money, and neither my age nor the colour of my hair would be of any consideration to them whatsoever.

*****

So Tanzania and many other countries in the tropics now enjoy a 'bottoms up' philosophy to play with. Every other aid vehicle has a logo painted brightly on the door. Dark-suited gentlemen and ladies sit majestically inside, going from one appointment to another.

Sometimes they are seen in the countryside driving in convoys viewing the various creations of their munificence, wells without water, schools without desks and books, irrigation systems silted up, pump stations without walls; clipboard analysis repeated yearly, 'What do you want? We can help.'

Photos adorn posh office walls. They, resplendent in shirt and tie, can be observed shaking hands with the many grateful recipients of their bounty; sweating profusely, soft and well-fed, pink in the midday sun, untutored in the ways of the tropics. Office-bound.

Today the theme 'bottoms up' drives the 'aid' disposal mission. Next time round it will probably be 'top down', and then, another decade later, perhaps 'sideways on', catchy ditties to unlock the rich nations' money boxes.

I was fortunate to have been involved during the early stages of this changing world of tropical agriculture but even then bureaucratic stumblings could hinder the progress of a project. But because the ditty then was 'hands on', the onus to success was placed firmly on our shoulders, allowing us a degree of freedom that nobody experiences now.

If Mr. Maugham was still around perhaps he would have written a sequel to his stories of tropical life. A chapter on dissolute planters revisited would be fitting and unfurl a thousand memories for those who knew and cared.